STARS MADE OF STORMS

A book with a life-enhancing impact on millions of people.

BINTE TAHIR

Printed in the Islamic Republic of Pakistan.

Printed: July, 2021
Edition: 1st
ISBN: 978-969-749-115-5
Price: Rs 1400 PKR, $14 US

www.auraqpublications.com | raabta@auraqpublications.com
@AuraqPublications | @AuraqBooks | +92-300-0571-530
Printed and Bound by *Passive Printers* - www.passiveprinters.com

For the creator whose trials even make us closer to Him.

Behind this enchanting book lie the true stories of many girls and boys who suffer alone, and become the warriors, the survivors. Obviously, the text is full of adventure, but it is set in a true-to-life situation, and thus achieves the perfect balance between being pleasurable to read and offering valuable lessons to learn.

TABLE OF CONTENT

GREY CLOUDS

Cramped, dim, and cave-like, a cheap, spindly pine framed bed cut shorter to fit into the room with a narrow carpet strip. To the right of the bed was a meanly proportioned window covered by twenty-something-year-old net curtains. The photographs had filled the walls. The floor was an old-fashioned parquet with a blend of deep homely browns.

She booted up her laptop, her eyes glazing over as the old device tried to connect to the internet. When it finally loaded, she was greeted with a collection of videos that YouTube recommended for her. She scrolled down, seeing more videos it wants her to watch, channels it thinks she would like. She clicks on one, and she was instantly sucked back into the never-ending, crimson world that is YouTube. She could watch anything from how-to videos to vlogs, from music videos to commercials.

The dance performance under the spotlight of the lady dancer was the life of the agora. Her sculpted figure was twin-thin, her waist tapered and the complexion glossy, slender eyebrows, velvety eyelashes, big blue eyes, sea nymph ears, dainty nose, and a set of dazzling, angle-white teeth, her ebony layered black hair which was same as her traditional layered clothing and virility-brown eyes that could set everyone's heart a-thump

If we see inside the bedroom through the window from the small lawn of that middle-class colony house, the room was filled with dull pale white light. She was lying on her front on the bed with her face down, seeing herself flickering on the screen of the laptop. Her dance video was uploaded on YouTube by some stranger just the day after her friend's birthday party where she did it. She didn't see the whole video but scrolled her phone's screen down. At first, her heart was filled with joy by reading the first few comments. She felt she could dance for the rest of her life, but as soon as she scrolled down more, people had highlighted 3:45 with the horrible comments. She scrolled up and started seeing the video again. When it reached 3:45, she turned red with anger; the one who had uploaded that had done much offensive editing in it. At that instance, she wanted it to be deleted from that unknown source.

She thought her heart will explode. Her eyes became wide with fear as she saw more. Her body wanted to run fast up to the hill for safety. She wanted to take one great leap off the pressure plate and run to safety.

Neck thickens, and breathing ceased,

And the body starts crumbling for ease.

She was almost going to vomit; she could taste saliva thickening in her throat and beads of sweat trickling down her brow. But at the same point, she thought that why was she afraid? She knew her father's saying that the right one is never afraid, so why was she afraid? Why did she fear? Was she wrong? No, she was not; she hadn't eaten pork or taken drugs, but if she wasn't wrong, so why was she afraid? She was frustrated and was having these sorts of miserable feelings until the pain took the place of fear. She found herself falling in the darkness. It was hard for her to breath. In the next few minutes, she was unconscious about the actual world.

She was sitting on the chair tied with the ropes in the hall's center, and the fire was burning in the fireplace. The dark orange-red fire burned a few iron rods, and the wax was boiling very next to her. A terrifying voice was coming continuously, saying all the rubbish comments. As she was near the flames, she could feel the heat. She was seeing the fire whose red embers were soaring in the black sky, its warmth increasing. She felt like her entire existence was burning in flames, and she woke up. It was a dream, a dreadful dream.

She became more scared because, for some unknown reason, old fears ran through her head when she heard the taunting laughter of years past when she was a fat kid and the punch line of teenage jokes.

As the painful memories play in the head,

Tears run down, shuddering hands reach the chest.

She was scared because those bad memories could invade her confidence. They would erode the person she had built since those dark days. The fear came and fled in the nighttime; she often vanquished it by the time she awoke. Still, this time she felt that she couldn't dominate that. Her thoughts tumbled into the fire and the boiling wax. She turned off her laptop and took a deep breath, waiting for something good, waiting for the helicopter which could take her out of there, and let it all go.

She suffered a week of a high fever. It was a benefit for her that her college had a summer break. As the college reopened, she felt a bit well.

******

Even the one who says good morning to everyone daily avoided greeting the group of gothically dressed teenagers who frequented the college's garden. Maybe because he has seen her video and thought the same as the people who expressed repulsive thoughts in the comments. Perhaps, he would be the one who has uploaded that video, but she doesn't know why? But he doesn't, and she notices that. They often walk along the balustrade, laughing loudly; they laughed the loudest! But what about her? Was she enjoying her friend's zone or was she in another world?

"Hey, Zany! In which world are you living?" said Insiya.

Insiya called her when they were roaming in the college garden, as she was walking separately in her own world of thoughts.

Her friends named her Zany, which is an excellent way to call her crazy, but she was named by her parents 'Zaini'. Zaini is an Arabic name that means beautiful or cheerful.

The fear traveled in Zaini's veins, but she was an excellent actress. She could hide that, but her eyes became steady, and her complexion became pale and matt. She let out a sigh and made herself prepared, showing that she wasn't afraid of anything. She was fine.

Insiya was Zaini's friend; she definitely wasn't the princess type. Her hair was barely combed back into a messy ponytail, and dirt was smeared across her cheek and forehead. With her t-shirt ripped and jeans caked with dried mud, there was never a moment when dust wasn't covering her. And she was perfectly okay with it. She thought that she looked cool in it, but who was gonna tell her the reality, as she couldn't listen to a single word against herself.

"Insiya, don't you know she lives on the earth? How stupid you are!" said Ahil jokingly, placing both hands in his jeans pocket.

Ahil, Zaini's classmate, Insia's first cousin, and her fiancé. He is never less than arrogant. He'd been brought up with the belief that he is superior to everyone. Perhaps, he could have been handsome, heroic even, but his sneer made him the ugliest damn thing. The day he became the CR was the day he left humanity for good; he became utterly toxic.

"Hey, you both stupids! Cut the crap; she looks upset and, you both are making fun," Aaira stopped them and went to Zaini.

Aaira is Zaini's friend. She has a distinctive personality. Her eyes speak of a beautiful soul, and she says so beautifully. She's not fair-toned, but the way she's comfortable in her own skin and bones makes her beautiful. She is the one who can laugh at anything, including herself, but at the right timings, she is kind, caring and a soft-hearted friend.

"Zaini, our Zany, it's awful to see you upset. What happened to you?" She asked with care.

"Nothing much. I'm just tired, there were guests yesterday, so I did much work. And then the assignment was left to do, so the burden became more, and I had completed it by staying awake whole night. I'm fine, no need to worry!" The lie slipped out, smooth and quick like melted butter running down toast; this is how she wins in satisfying her.

*****

"I'll be honest now," she said to herself.

She was pretty glad when the first six months were over. She had been doing her introductory teacher training course for the last six months after returning from college. Now she thought she had got to the grueling bit. She was halfway through the training, but with a challenging uphill slog to go before she got to the finish line by the end of the year.

Eliza and Zaini met before and after classes and often sat on the river banks talking late into the night.

Eliza is Zaini's best friend and an Asthma patient. She values Zaini above all her friends and, of course, Zaini also. They do much fun with each other, and Eliza is the rare one Zaini trusts, the first person she calls when she gets good news or a bad one. She is her sunshine. And so it is always light in her world, in the sweet, velvety nights, even in the inky and perfect black, whatever the circumstances are, she is by her side without any exception. Her friendship is a light to her that somehow grows inside her soul and shines through her own eyes.

When Zaini started, she was the junior trainee, the group's baby, with plenty of room for error and a human shield made up of senior-level students. Time has passed, those students have moved on, and she is now a senior trainee with no more room for error.

"Roll no. 36, Zaini, come here and take your useless assignment for God's sake. I have not that much time to waste on your poor assignment," Miss Mirha screamed; her harshness was relentless.

Miss Mirha, Zaini's new teacher, is already obese and triple inflated (don't know who, but someone blind, has given her this job). She is quite insufferable, jealous of her because of her figure flexibility grades, which she gets always. If she rarely does any wrong yoga posture, Miss Mirha gets a chance to use her as an example of how not to do a yoga pose.

"Yes, Miss, coming," said Zaini tiredly, "Oh Miss Zoya, one week is so much. Please come in a day, please please please, or else this beast will chew me raw; she is viciously wicked," she said to herself, asking Miss Zoya to come for help.

Miss Zoya, an ideal yoga teacher who touches her students' hearts in every way; the one students could never get better than. She warms her students' hearts by the way she teaches and has the ability to cater to both beginners and advanced students at the same time. She is a certified yoga instructor who focuses more on their students for becoming happier students. She teaches with the passion of a lifelong teacher, someone who lives to inspire a love of learning in the next generation.

Zaini's final written assignment was handed back to her by her new yoga teacher no less than five times, covered in scribbles and corrections. She saw her so-called useless assignment by Miss Mirha and threw it in the trash.

She was walking in the passage of the training center. It was straight like a drinking straw and almost as narrow. There was a weird strain that filled the environment. She kicked the garbage with each stride; the stress had peripheralized her. After a few steps, there was a room; she stepped inside as she knew it was the dressing room and there was no one inside.

She walked with downcast eyes, and her thick bangs almost reached her nose. Her clothes were tight, as they need to be, sleeveless shirt and yoga pants. She had spent half of the day in stress or anxiety or whatever it was called. She sat down on the floor, trying to control her breathing and prevent her face from turning beet red. But the breaths came quicker, and her cheeks warmed regardless. She knew that if she cried, her face would be puffy and scorching. In a split of seconds, she took the decision, stood up, went to the basin, washed her face, took out the water bottle from her bag, drank a lot of water, took deep breaths, and inhaled and exhaled. Now it's time to go.

"Hello, Sir Kaif! May I come in?" Zaini asked while standing at Sir Kaif's office door.

Under the artificial glow of the strip lighting, Sir Kaif was more pale than usual. Everything about him was otherwise typical. It was the same old polyester suit and same grey tie with a black stripe. His hair was a comb-over, and his front teeth were reconstructed after an accident with a lawnmower. His smile was as genuine as a car salesman and only worn for special occasions.

When he spoke, everyone listened. He aspired to confidence by being competent and showing a willingness to listen.

The office was painted grey, and it had only one floor-to-ceiling window, which faced the main road. On the grey desk sat a desktop computer, a notebook lying open, and the stack of papers sitting under a cute-creature paperweight. In a corner, the air conditioner was blasting at medium, and there was a pirouette chair in the middle. A bookshelf bursting with books was in the corner, yet another stack of papers under paperweight was shaped like a tuft of grass. A few pens were lying on the documents; maybe he was busy.

"Yes, sure, come in," he looked up and said.

"Thank you, Sir. Are you busy?" asked Zaini respectfully while standing in front of him.

"A bit, but you come in and have a seat, kid," he said while moving the chair forward to her, "Have any problem?"

His saying her a 'kid' made her feel something so good that she couldn't explain. He always discovers this significant way of communicating emotions; he finds the right words.

Of course, words can lift us up or tear us down. They can build, and they can destroy. Words can encourage or stop us in our tracks. Words can put us on the right path or point to a dark end. Words can reveal the truth or they can hide the fact. Words can be weapons or they can be tools to build our self-worth. Some words may fade away quickly while others hit with the impact of a wrecking ball and lodges in the memory. He handles words with great care.

"Yes, Sir, I need a few days of leave," she said with her heart accelerating.

"Okay, I will grant you, but I'm seeing your report for this week is not good. If there is any problem, you could share! Are you okay?" he asked the question smoothly.

The baritone of his voice reverberated through Zaini's bones. The low rumble of his voice was comforting as it wrapped around Zaini and carried her off to a world where the sound was the power that could change everything wrong in the world.

"I'm fine," she pips.

In a minute, she realized that Sir Kaif was waiting for an answer, the actual answer.

"Sir, actually I'm not feeling well nowadays. I need some days of rest," her heart melted as the snow melts at the beginning of the summer. She wanted to tell him everything that was going on in her head, but, "No, never," she said to herself.

The worst situation is when

Your heart is craving,

But you remain silent.

Your brain is screaming,

But the tongue remains dormant.

"Okay," he said while shaking his head in affirmation, "So when will you come then?"

"In a week, Sir."

"Okay, have some rest and come back with perfect health; take care."

"Thank you, Sir," she said while standing up from the chair.

"You're welcome," he replied pleasantly. They both exchanged smiles, and then Zaini went out. She was leaving, but in truth, it was an escape, emancipation.

There comes a time when your voice has been so cramped up inside of you that you need to break out or risk breakdown. Zaini took a deep breath as she got a week's break to encourage herself to come back to life.

She is not going to come back again to this place, but who knows?

*****

"It's a baby freeze,

Trying to do a baby freeze.

And when your hands go down,

Lift your legs up!

Now take your right elbow.

And put it in your side,

Keep it close to your belly button,

Put it to your side!

Now take your left hand,

And put it down on the ground.

That's called your power arm,

Down on the ground!

Lift one leg up,

You can do it with ease.

Lift the other leg up,

When I count to three!"

There was a light upon that wooden floor that danced and played as the feet of happy children might.

She was watching her students' moves with glee. She stood with a hip jutted to one side, her right arm draped across her slender body, clasping the elbow opposite. Her head lolled down to one shoulder, casting her ebony layered hair onto the shirt that was too tight. Every one of her students was chuffed in, landing their hands and lifting their legs with the rhythm of the music so much that they didn't saw their Zaini, Ma'am Zaini.

"Abeeha, you are folding your knee; keep it straight and firm."

Everyone stopped and moved behind to see who said that, as it was not the mam's time to come.

"Hello, Ma'am!" They all said together, a small smile played on their lips.

They were glad to see their mam early.

"Hello, students, what were you all doing?" She asked.

"We were practicing the moves you had taught us yesterday," said Mishal.

"Oh, good, but...today, I'm giving you early off because I am going to take your test tomorrow, so practice at home. I will give you the remarks according to your performance," told Mam Zaini

"Okay, Ma'am, Goodbye," they all said together and went.

"Ma'am, I want to tell you something." Abeeha stopped at the door and said to Zaini.

"Yes, yes, say whatever you want to, Kid." said Zaini (She didn't forget Sir Kaif calling her a 'kid,' this word was quite relaxing. Obviously, teachers are the one who leave their precious words for their students to gain something good in every phase of life.)

"Ma'am, your words are like vanilla pudding, sweet in an ordinary sort of way. The richness of your tone is luxurious and warm. You must be a baritone in church. I'm glad I have a teacher like you," said Abeeha. She loved her teacher, and of course, a teacher is always the loveliest to the students.

Zaini held her cheeks with her hands, lifted her face up, and said,

"Dear Kiddo, thank you, but I bet you wanted to say something else!"

"Abeeha, come on, hurry up. I'm waiting for you outside, watcha doin' there?" shouted Mishal.

"Maybe," murmurs Abeeha.

"You may go right now. Come a bit earlier tomorrow, then we will talk, okay!" she said with care.

"Okay, Ma'am, Goodbye," she said happily and went.

But who has seen tomorrow? Who knows tomorrow's fate?

The conversation was so much more than anything that is so beloved to Abeeha. It is the smile, the gentle shrugs, and the light in the eyes, her elevation by her mam's presence that was apparent, and even the silences were comfortable. They were the moments to savor the company and feel that sense of peace that comes from feeling loved and protected within the presence of her.

The stale evening was turning into night, and the darkness was spreading all over the city.

Zaini was like a boat at sea in her childhood, searching for a safe harbor in every storm. Then she realized that she had become the harbor and she could provide shelter to others.

*****

She was sitting on the chair tied with the ropes in the hall's center; the fire was burning in the fireplace. The dark orange-red fire burns a few iron rods, and the wax was boiling very next to her. A terrifying voice coming continuously that was saying all the rubbish comments. As she was near the flame, she could feel the heat. She was seeing the fire whose red embers were soaring in the black sky, its warmth increasing. She was feeling like her entire existence was burning in flames, and she woke up from the same dream.

She stood up from the floor as she had sat there leaning against the door. She checked the time. It was 3:30; the room has been swallowed by the darkness. She went to the bathroom.

The bathroom had an earthy feel. The walls were large format tiles of white honed travertine. The floor was made of dull brown tiles, and the vanities were of dark wood.

She saw her face in the mirror. It was entirely red. She turned on the faucet. A rain-like sound was echoing within the walls of the bathroom, yet each drop was alone as it fell. Zaini stayed still, eyes resting on the waterfall as they had been for the past minutes, her mind slowly telling her that she needs to wash her face. She plunged her hands under the icy stream of water and gasped.

She washed her face, washed and washed and washed so much that her clothes became wet. She came outside and lay on the bed.

She opened her video by clicking on the YouTube app icon. She had no courage to see that again, so she decided to report that video. Successfully after a few minutes, her video was not on YouTube anymore. Now she thinks everything will gonna be okay, but who knows?

She checks her WhatsApp. There were 23 messages. She opened them one by one. A total of twenty-one messages were the group chats, memes, and videos that she didn't like at all, and the twenty-second one was the most dreadful for her. It was of Abeeha's and Mishal's mother. It said:

"WE ARE HAVING A NEW HOME SO FAR FROM YOURS, SO I CAN'T SEND ABEEHA AND MISHAL TO YOU ANYMORE."

The tears came out of her eyes once again on the same night.

"Now, how many incidents are left to happen that will give me definitely the pain?" she asked herself.

"No money, no cure, no cure, no health, no health, more diseases, more diseases, more pain, more pain, less courage, less courage, less life, less life, no dad..."

She jerked off her head, wiped the tears, and continued reading the next message. It was of Abrash's, Sofia's, and Yafiah's mother. It said:

"I CAN'T SEND ABRASH, SOFIA, AND YAFIAH ANYMORE. BECAUSE OF THE DANCE PRACTICE, THEY ARE NOT ABLE TO FOCUS ON THEIR ACADEMIC STUDIES AS THEY ARE HAVING MUCH BURDEN. THEY NEED TO PAY FULL ATTENTION."

The only five students and the only hope for money, which was no more. "What should I do now?" she questioned herself. "Blood transfusion could save your daddy, but first, pay the advance," she revised the doctor's saying. "I have to pay the college's new semester fees, I have to clear the yoga classes charges, I have to bring the medicines, what will I do now? Ughhh!!! What will I do now? Why the adversities come over to me always?" Her muscles ached. She was crying and sobbing. She kept questioning herself, seeking the logical part of the answer. The vicious cycle of recalling every recollection and replaying it had begun, and the question remained: "Why?"

When you feel your life is a thunderstorm,
And you can't see the sunshine;
When you are fuckingly feeling bad
And don't know how to express,
When you need to ask yourself,
Why always me!

LITTLE BY LITTLE

Felicie was sweeping the stage. She sighed deeply while looking at the ballet shoes, and Camille once again stealed her music box.

"Leave it. Give it back," said Felicie.

Camille chuckled and said, "Silly me. I didn't throw it hard enough THE FIRST TIME."

She prepared to throw it across the room, but Felicie grabbed her wrist and took the music box back.

"Don't make the same mistake," Felicie warned and took a few steps forward from her.

"Why are you leaving? Scared of being humiliated?"

Felicie stopped and faced her. "Looks like you need more training." She used her broom to stretch her body. "You're nowhere near ready."

She dropped her broom as she and Camille circled each other on tiptoes.

"I'm going to show you what a real dancer looks like," challenged Camille.

"Are you sure about that?" Felicie smiled mischievously.

"Quiet! Tonight, these seats will be full! Paris will be looking at ME! Adoring ME!" said Camillie while pointing at the opera seats.

Felicie smirks, "Or not".

"I have already told you! You are nothing! You will always be nothing!" said Camille furiously.

Felicie span up to her, "Only one way to find out. Right here. Right now."

Felicie and Camille engaged in a dance-off. Nora walked in and noticed.

"Oh my God," Nora pleasantly surprised.

She rushed out of the room and shouted to the others in

the building, "DANCE-OFF!"

Zaini shouted when Nora shouted, and when they both shouted, dad shouted, and the whole cinema shouted!

"DANCE-OFF!"

The cheers erupted like an auditory volcano and came with fists in the air and eyes flung wide. It was all quiet one second and then deafening the next. They all were electrified, awake, soaring to new heights of emotion. Felicie's achievement made every one of them want to get on the track, to train. If she could do it, so could they. Maybe not at first, but didn't they all suck at new things until they practiced?

When they both came out after seeing Zaini's favorite animated movie 9th time, that was Leap, Zaini asked, "Do you know I often see a dream, and today also, I saw that. Are you willing to listen, Dad?"

"Yes, sure!" he answered.

"Okay! I took about five running steps and leaped into the air. Assuming the pose of superman, I flew over dales and rivers right to the coast and over the cliffs. Barely skimming the waves, I headed into the horizon and the setting sun, then without warning, I plunged into the ocean. I could breathe, and I was as fast below the surface as I had been on top. The fish swam around me in a myriad of colors, shapes, and sizes. Then I met with a blue whale who told me of their sorrow in his sing-song trills, which somehow made total sense, and sent me back to the land. And after taking five running steps, I leaped into my bed, and so I wake up."

"Oh, fascinating dream! So your dream started with a leap and ended the same. Were you like Felicie?"

"Yes, Dad," she said. "Dad, I will become a ballerina like Felicie when I grow up," she said while looking in his eyes and holding his hand tightly with both her hands in an insisting manner.

"Like Felicie," he asked with his wandering gaze.

"Yes, Yes, Dad, like Felicie," she said with excitement.

"Oh, don't you say that."

"Why not, Dad?" she asked in a childish, emotional way.

"She was an orphan. Are you?"

"Oh, come on, Dad, don't talk like a kiddo."

"Hahaha," he laughed at the way she said KIDDO.

"I will jump longer than Felicie did, and then you will be proud."

"Yes, of course, I will be proud."

"Dad?" She looked at him demurely.

"Yes."

"Do we get money in doing ballet?" She was serious now.

"Yes, a lot of money, but why are you asking me so?"

"I will earn a lot of money and then will give half of that to the needy, orphans, and the sick who don't have enough money to cure themselves."

"Oh, great thinking, Honey. I am proud to have a kind-hearted daughter like you." He appreciated her, clung, and kissed her. She kissed him in return.

"I can get a lot of money in ballet. Yes, Father, I can get. I will arrange your blood transplant, and you will be fit once again," she said to herself when she became conscious about the present world.

She had traveled to her childhood when she was 10 and had gone with her dad to the movie theatre to see her favorite movie. It may seem a small thing, but those days, dad was so busy. Somehow, he was in crisis; she didn't know what had happened precisely with him as he never told.

"Animated movies were my drug of choice. In the choreographed moments, directed by the greats and acted by legends, I am still free to explore my dark side. I root for the hero and enjoy the sick logic of the villain. I'm self-confessed that I am a 'movies junkie.' I have become the genius of filmography, and the real world drifts away as if it was the fictional world and the movies are my new reality," she was talking with herself, reminiscing about her childhood hobbies.

Zaini loved the movies and the cinemas too. Even though no matter how much she grew up, she could feel like the ten-year-old Zaini who became excited while walking through the cinema's door and seeing the big screen. Who got there early enough to snag her favorite seat, then sit there hugging her family-sized popcorn until the film began. Who allowed her a few slurps of pop in the trailer and then ate the rest in the whole movie.

Dad loved Zaini so much that he accepted all her wishes whether legal or illegal. She found herself recollecting about that time when they ate popcorn and enjoyed the movie in each other's company.

The happy memory unfolds as the pages of a beloved childhood storybook. These are the happy memories that sustain us, that carry us through the challenging times of loss, and remind us that our loving is essential and worthwhile. They come as a welcomed stranger through the door, suddenly present and lighting up the room with a smile.

*****

No one knows how the dark night has changed itself into a shiny morning that brings a new freshness to the light as if the world has been upgraded to some higher definition.

She had laid with her head on the bed. Her phone was ringing beside her. It was 6:30 am, and the alarm was ringing. The alarm buzzer went off like an annoyed rattlesnake, but that day, she decided to be absent in the college no matter how much Miss Aiza would scold her. For her dad's life, she could bear everything.

Zaini swiped her screen's phone with a lot of exhaustion to snooze the alarm. She turned her face towards the roof and kept thinking of what to do. She only had some dance skills that she could earn money from, but she didn't know about any dance agency. Miss Zoya could help her, but she didn't have her number and she would not come, of course, to the yoga class as she had gone abroad. “Now who’s left to ask for help,” she wondered.

The thought trundled through her brain like a train, with no intention of stopping.

She was thinking that she was gradually losing her father. Each door of help was closed, no route led to success, success of curing her dad.

She had come to her father (she calls her grandfather just father), crying bitterly. She kept saying, "There is nothing worse than homework. There is no way to solve it. I will never get good marks because of this disgusting sum. It's impossible to solve this; no one can do this, and there is no one for help." She had kept doing nonsense, and her father was listening to that. He was the only one who always listened to her bunk. She did her nonsense only in front of him (A beautiful relation!). When she became silent, he said;

"The helping door is never closed, and the helper is always with us. He can do everything. He is the biggest, we just need to follow what He says, and our life will be successful," he said in a restful manner.

"But there is no one to help me except you," she argued. "Are you saying of yourself that you are with me for help every time?" she asked.

He shook his head. "I go to the market; I go to the relatives' homes. I don't go with you to your school; I'm not with you always."

"Then who is with me always?" she inquired.

"The Creator of everything."

That was the soft-spoken word she never heard before. It sounded like a drum, but deeper, like a tuba. Father's tone was as deep as the moon at midnight. It's low and soft but powerful enough to send chills through the body.

"And who is the creator of everything?" She was having a keen interest in his talks.

Maybe mother had listened that she was talking to her father. She came, squeezed her shoulders, took her to her room, and started slapping and beating her. She could only scream. Mother shoved the table, destroying the glass vase, and the glass shattered everywhere. She then pulled Zaini down to the floor...her back sticking on the glass pieces, and then violently started beating her. She could do nothing but burst into tears. She did not even say a single word, as she had no courage. She just kept screeching and crying. Feeling her shoe going through her stomach, she couldn't take the pain anymore, "Stoppp, pleeease, pleeease, just stoppp.!" she was squealing...

When you need to ask why me

And you want to move freely;

When you don't know what to do,

And your closest become against you.

Those wounds and broken bones had cured, but one thing didn't for sure: the scars on her heart. The mother that she loved did that awful thing. She couldn't even believe it. She had beaten her that hard just because she was talking to father!

She loved her father as same as she loved her dad. She always obeyed him though her mother wanted to keep her daughter away from him, why? She never knew.

She had spent a summer with her father when her laughter was as the daisies in the grass. She also spent a winter with him and she felt as if ice froze her heart and blood. For her, he was the shelter, the guardian, the forever home, but why is he not with her anymore? She doesn't know.

The days spent with father were the days of bright sunshine, blue skies that sung of the summer to come. They were the days of cloud-filtered rays, the ones that made the world so cozy.

Those were the days when it began to rain, instead of dashing inside, she stayed in the garden to dance, to taste that feast of water, but they WERE the days!

She had gone to her childhood again when she had failed in doing the kindergarten math sum the 7th time, she was crying bitterly. When grandfather started to tell her exciting things, her mother took her away from him. She beat her and warned her to not to talk with him or else the consequence would be more dreadful.

She never forgets her grandfather's sayings whether she is with him or not. She believes everything he told her.

"THE HELPING DOOR IS NEVER CLOSED, AND THE HELPER IS ALWAYS EVERY TIME WITH US; HE CAN DO EVERYTHING. HE IS THE BIGGEST."

She still remembers her grandfather's saying. He said that there is a helper. He never speaks rubbish, so there is, but who? She asked herself.

She kept questioning herself.

"THE HELPER IS ALWAYS, EVERY TIME, WITH US!"

She was repeating this sentence as she felt that there is something deep inside.

"If the helper is everywhere, so the helper is with me here right now?" she repeated her sentence with alertness as something had knocked her.

"Can you see me?"

"Can you hear me?"

She asked aloud. No one answered, but she still believes that the biggest helper is there.

"So the biggest one,

Please let this burden fall.

Take the world off my shoulders.

I am not one of the soldiers.

(She thought of the poetry she wrote months before.)

"My grandfather told me about you. He said to me that there is a helper always. If you are the helper, please help me in searching for a job so that I would have money for my father's treatment."

She was saying it aloud as she was feeling that someone was genuinely listening to her. She thought that the beam of hope was falling on her.

She felt as if the weight lifted from her shoulders, as if an overly large child had just leaped off after a satisfying piggyback ride. She walked taller. Her stride was lighter, more carefree. She noticed how the white light of the morning streamed in through her room's window. A girlish grin spread onto her red cheeks as she burst into the waiting summer morning like a blackbird's melody.

*****

"Oh, woooah, oh

Wooooah, oh

Wooooah, oh..."

From somewhere came the sound of an old-fashioned telephone, so authentic that Zaini scanned the room for that antique. She moved around the room. After a few moments, she stopped at the heavy wooden table and slid her hand underneath. There was something taped there in plastic. Zaini ducked down, peeling away dusted duct tape to release the package, still ringing. It was a telephone, the oldest model. She ripped the plastic bag with her incisors and pulled it out.

"Hello," she said.

"Hello, Zany, were you awake or did I disturb you?"

She could recognize the voice. Why couldn't she, as it was of whom she never forgets.

"No, no, I was awake, but it's 7:04. How are you awake? Or haven't you slept yet?" she inquired while staring at the wristwatch.

Eliza laughed and said, "You know me well. I didn't sleep."

"Why?" She was amazed as she thought she only keeps awake at night.

"Do you remember I had told you months before that I am going to work as a personal secretary of the manager of the dance academy?"

"Yes, yes, so? Did you get the job?" she became excited.

"Yes, but there is a problem, and all I need is you."

"Oh", her heart started beating faster than before. "What's the problem? I will help you as deep as I could."

"Thank you", she expressed gratitude, "So yes, they have given me the job, but they are finding a director for the neoclassical ballet for so long that now if someone with my reference comes, they will give me the bonus and all I think of you. Can you do the directory?"

She took a deep breath and thought of the things she said with the one who is the biggest, who is the helper. Does He listen to her in real or was it only an incident? She was confused.

"Yes, of course, but when to go?"

"Just today, right now!" said Eliza, smilingly.

"What? Right now?" she was appalled.

"Yes, right now, couldn't you come?"

"Yes, I could, but..."

"My sis, don't you have any manners? Your friend is standing outside the door, and you are not opening it!"

"What!"

Zaini threws the handset, washed her face, as it was still red, rushed downstairs, and opened the gate. Both exchanged smile when they saw each other.

"Such a big surprise," said Zaini.

"It should be, Dear," replied Eliza, "Won't you invite me inside?"

"Of course, Zany do!"

"Zany? Is this you?" Her father woke up by the noise they were making.

"Oh, maybe dad has awakened," she whispered.

"Yes, Dad, and Eliza is also here."

"Your friend Eliza! I do remember her; offer her some snacks and tea," he advised.

"Yes, Dad!" she replied.

"Hey, you girl! I will give you the snacks because Dad said so, but indeed, you don't deserve," she smirks. "Now will you come in or do I need to pick you up in my arms?... But no! You would be so heavy I couldn't."

"No, no, you couldn't pick up a smart-looking girl," she smirks in exchange while taking a step inside the house.

"Thank God you came in!" said Zaini, and Eliza smiled in return.

*****

They both sat on the couch of her room. There was a little space between them where Zaini placed some snacks and tea. Before that, Eliza took off her coat and hung it on Zaini's wall hanger, pulled out the key split ring from her finger and hung it on the key holder, took off her handbag and place it beside her as it was her home and she was relaxed.

Eliza had a designer handbag, perfect cerise stitching over the finest creamy-hued Italian leather. The cotton trims matched both the thread and the exact shade of the lipstick she wore, but from deep within the straining sides always came a faint rattle, as if she never traveled without pills of some kind.

The beautifully designed couch in the living room has seen many years, many seasons. The leather has worn past that is the point of distress, and now there are small tears and holes. The once bright tan color has been bleached by the sun that streams in the window. The hue is now a warm, soft beige. Eliza pokes her finger into a hole and wiggles it; underneath is a white foam that hasn't seen daylight in almost twenty years. She pulls her finger out and turns to let herself eat some snacks with a good thump.

In those summer days, the iced tea was a blessing, and it felt so divine holding the teacup after refrigerating it for a while.

Eliza took a double take, her lengthy hair swishing over her face. The biscuits were not just any kind: custard creams and bourbons. It took a half-second to remember that she wasn't a child anymore and that asking for one wasn't the done thing. Then with a tender bite of her inner lip, she split them in half, eating the dry side first, savoring the half with the cream filling. Her inner voice found some volume. "May I have a biscuit, please? I haven't seen these kinds of biscuits since I was a teenager."

"Have some more biscuits; who are you waiting for?" asked Zaini.

"I am waiting for you!" said Eliza with a smile (Thanks for asking me. Yes, I could eat all of them though I am not hungry, but, Girl, I could), she said to herself.

"For me! Sounds odd."

"Yes, for you. It sounds odd because you know you don't deserve it," replied Eliza mischievously

"No one can win from you," Zaini reacted that she was fed up with her, but deep down, she wasn't.

"You are so right. Thank you for admiring it."

Eliza and Zaini always argue with each other, but they are never serious. They just do it for fun, and they both know that very well.

"So, what were you talking about the job?" asked Zaini seriously.

"Oh, yes, I was saying that I need you for the directory of neoclassical ballet, but there is another problem."

"What?"

"Sir Zayan's neoclassical ballet academy is in India. I will be with you there as I am his secretary, and for going there, we need some money."

“No way! money again,” she said to herself. "How much?" she asked soberly.

"Approx. 1 lakh."

"And how much we will get?"

"It's a big amount!"

"Are you sure?"

"Yes, approx. 10 lakh!"

She became happy by listening to the amount, as indeed she needed that, "Hmm, I do agree; when to go?"

"Just today, just right now!" Eliza smiled, and Zaini smiled in return.

*****

Eliza was driving the car; the traffic was much. People were rushing their cars and motorbikes, as it was the office timings.

The road stretches onward, embracing the land, taking each turn in comfortable stride. It is a grey that has welcomed many suns and becomes silvery as it soaks in the rays.

Zaini let her eyes run over each hue, seeing black blemishes for the first time yet feeling the details created by an artistic hand. They render it all the more beautiful.

Eliza was gazing straight ahead. The traffic wound its way down the road like a tremendous angry snake, tires hissing over the road.

It was the most popular cafe street of the city. People were going to do breakfast mostly with their loved ones and were parking their cars with a disorder, like a road was owned by them and it was theirs and theirs alone.

Eliza puzzled whether to drive on the right lane, left lane, or in the center. The car moving in front of them moved on the left sometimes, sometimes on the right, or in the center. She was following that car as obeying the driving rule.

She came beside that car with a lot of struggle, and all she could realize was how wonderfully fool she had become. It took her a minute to realize that she was just chasing rainbows because on the right mirror of the back seat, "L" was written in bold, which means learning, and they didn't need to follow a learning driver.

"April fool!" said Zaini with a laugh.

"It's not 1st April, please," she said with a low tune that seemed she was fed up with the traffic and her will was to eat the driver raw.

"Hey, Eliza! It's 'Cafe Foodies,' and I have heard about a great deal. It's relatively inexpensive and serves a good breakfast. Let's go there first," Zaini was just diverting her exhausted mind.

"Oh, Yes, I have also heard about it."

"So, who are you waiting for? There's the space; just rush there so no one could park as there is only one car parking space left," said Zaini while pointing her finger to the cafe's parking lot.

Eliza holds the clutch, moves the gear into the first mode, and revs the engine at around 2,000-4,000 rpm. She disengages the clutch all of a sudden, not gently, and presses the accelerator.

In the cartoons, when someone moves so fast, all they leave is a blurred trail of color. That's how it was with Eliza when she rushed her car on the road.

She had parked the car a minute later, as they both came out from the car and closed the door. The driver of the same vehicle that fooled them was looking at them with hope. They both moved towards the cafe and acted as they didn't see him.

Square tables, glass tops with the menu under them, slow-turning ceiling fans above, large windows, luxury vinyl tiled floor, light classical music, small vases of yellow carnation flowers on each table, daily specials on a chalkboard at the entrance, and waiters smartly dressed in black and white!

They both placed their bags on the table, pulled the chair, and sat. The counter was near, and the table beside them was empty—that was the best place.

A minute later, a group of boys came laughing and gossiping and sat on that empty table. Eliza and Zaini were looking at each other, both thinking the same. A few minutes later, the boys got attentive to them. They were seeing them repeatedly and were exchanging mischievous smiles in their circle. It seems their energy spilled out just as much as the coffee in their cups, and every other noise was their laughter. “If she didn't need money, she would never have come here,” thought Zaini.

They both were unable to bear the tawdry boys' acts more. Therefore, they stood up, picked up their bags, and walked fast towards the door.

"Ma'am! Ma'am, your order! Where are you going?" one of the boys said.

Zaini stopped, faced him, and said, "No, we don't need it!" and walked towards the door as Eliza had bumped into a boy there.

"May I help you?" he said while giving a big artificial smile, and till then, Zaini reached there.

"No," Zaini pushed him away, held Eliza's hand tightly and walked fast toward the car.

They both were surrounded by fear, the fear of being caught. They were feeling the screaming of their lungs and the will of their muscles to go far. This was the body and brain in full survival mode, and they were having nothing but pain.

They sat in the car. The boys were coming towards them, but Eliza pushed the turbo button and rushed to the road. They both were mutely sitting like they had been smelled by a snake.

"Thank God!" Eliza broke the silence.

"But our order?" Zaini composed herself and said while acting emotionally.

"Just leave it, Sis!" said Eliza.

"Yes, I have left!" said Zaini with a cheerful voice.

It seemed that even they didn't want to discuss anything that had happened anymore.

"And here we are!" said Eliza while stopping the car in front of the giant board on which it was written, "Welcome to the dance academy."

A boy guard came. Eliza rotated the crank handle to open the window and showed him the card.

The boy saw the card, said, "Welcome to dance academy," and they went inside.

*****

They both were in 'dance academy,' which would not be less valuable than Clifton, an affluent seaside municipality of Karachi.

The academy was built like a town. The streets were glorious in their inception. The sidewalks were smooth grey stone, joined with such precision that the joints were almost invisible. The walls were concrete, but not like a villa in rural Spain. They were more like the construction of modern buildings, sharp edges, and corners.

Zaini raised her head out the window to look, and what she saw stole her breath. The ground below her was alive with lights like someone had taken a handful of glitter and thrown it as far as the eyes could see.

There was a cluster of five buildings. The buildings were large with smoked glass; each one joined to the next by a covered walkway. There was a big central building which was not smaller than a skyscraper. That was the main building as there was the manager's office.

They entered. A boy came and asked, when they were standing at the entrance door, "May I help you? Where do you want to go?"

"We wanted to meet Sir Zayan," replied Eliza.

"What's your name?" asked the boy respectfully.

"Eliza!"

"Okay!" he said and went to the intercom.

"Hey, Eliza! Will he easily hire me as a director!" whispered Zaini.

"I'm full of hope! But why are you having this sort of question at this serious moment, Stupid!"

"You stupid! I'm just asking because of his richness; rich people are usually arrogant."

"No, Zaini, I have talked to him before. He is not arrogant, he is a soft-hearted and smooth-natured man. Have good hope, and everything will be good."

"Ma'am! Sir Zayan is waiting for you; come with me. I will take you to him," the boy came and said when Eliza spoke to Zaini.

"Okay!" Eliza nodded her head and signaled Zaini to follow.

The windows were made all over the building. It was so large that it reminded her of the cafe front. It was triple-glazed and so clear that the panorama was like a high-definition screen at the movie theatre. The birds were traveling past, buffeted by the winds that whistled through the buildings. The building in the sky felt so futuristic. The city below was so far away; it's like another world with ant-like people. All that building was her cocoon, and the window— well, the window showed Zaini as much detail as she wanted to know.

After a minute's walk, they were standing in front of the office's door.

"Here you are!" remarked the boy.

"Thank you!" said Eliza.

Eliza knocked on the door first. Zaini stood next to Eliza, who was staring at the door, unmoving.

"Come in, Eliza; I know it's you," a voice came from the other side.

The door opened wide to show a welcoming mat. It was pristine as if the indignity of a dirty shoe had never been placed upon it.

"Thank you!"

"Sit here!" said Zayan said while pointing at the chairs.

*****

Zaini was wearing jeans and a tank top with high heels while Eliza was in a long coat with casual loose pants. They both sat on the chairs.

A vast room occupied the corner of the building with floor-to-ceiling windows giving views in two directions: Fifth Avenue to the east, Central Park just a few blocks north. The two remaining walls contained a door, a low bookshelf, a single oil painting, and a flower vase. There was also a private elevator that opened directly into his office.

His desk's black glass surface was equally uncluttered: a computer, a leather notebook, and a framed photograph of a fourteen-year-old boy.

Sir Zayan was as grey as the linoleum. His suit was crisp, his shirt ironed to perfection, and he was wearing a white tie with a pink stripe.

"Sir, this girl," Eliza pointed toward Zaini, "is perfectly fitted for the job of the director of neoclassical ballet!"

"Hmm, how could you prove to me that she is the perfect one?" asked Sir Zayan.

They both sneaked a look and asked what to answer, as they both hadn't expected such a question from him.

"How can I prove?" asked Zaini calmly.

"You came here for the directory, and in return, I will pay you money. So, giving money is my headache and proving is yours!" he said in a stiff and formal tone.

"Sorry, I don't get you," apologized Zaini, "Can you guide me?"

"What's your name?"

"Zaini."

"So, Miss Zaini, I am describing you in a few words which I Hope you will understand," said Sir Zayan, "If you came here thinking that I need a director, change your thinking just right now because I don't need you; I want you."

"How could you just say that..." Zaini was amazed.

"Miss Zaini! What do you think of your clothes? My courage of speaking gained after seeing you," he sarcastically remarked while overviewing her from tip to toe. Zaini could feel the bitterness of his words in her throat. Eliza was listening to them in a silent mode. "You would get money in exchange, don't forget," he added. He had stupefied her; she felt the ground slipping under her feet.

"Miss Zaini," he made her aware while clenching both his hands together and resting them on the desk. "The ball is in your court."

"Okay, that's just fine!" surrendered Zaini.

"Wait for the night!" he said sarcastically.

"Fine!" she said while standing up from her chair.

Eliza stood with her. Sir Zayan offered Zaini a hand to shake. The hand Zaini provided in return was manicured to perfection; the skin was softer than baby girls. He smiled like a long-lost brother and shook Zaini's hand warmly with the perfect squeeze and eye contact. Zaini reciprocated.

"Nice to meet you. You could go wherever you want, but remain here in this academy," he said while mentioning his dance academy. Zaini nodded her head in affirmation.

"Eliza, you go with her and guide her on everything. She is our chief guest!" commanded Zayan with roguishness.

This was the second time Eliza found Sir Zayan attentive to her in that long conflict, which she had not understood truly. She was just in the silent mode, seeing both faces silently.

'Okay, Sir!" she said with obedience, as obedience was the only thing she could do. She was his secretary.

*****

THE END OF WAITING HOURS

Abeeha reached out towards the curtain and drew it aside in one firm motion. Beyond the curtains of that high-class room of an elite-class house, she couldn't even see the glass in that brilliant light of March. The sun streams in like a flamboyant guest, not waiting for an invitation.

She was the kind of girl girls loved to hate. She was a teenager yet going to be an adult as she was 19—but so young that she still exhibited youth's exuberance. She had that movie star look, not overly tall and willowy but more like an action star. Her muscle definition was perfect, and she walked with the confidence of someone a decade older. She wasn't just flawless in her bone structure; her black skin was also utterly flawless.

You are not your dull complexion,

Nor the body size you have.

She was all about simplicity, making things easy, helping those around her, relaxed and happy with what she had. Perhaps that is why her skin glowed; it was her inner beauty that lit her eyes and softened her features. To be in her company was to feel that you too were someone, that you had been warmed in summer rays regardless of the season.

You are the sweetener of your words,

And the harshness of your speech.

She had seen the postman from the window riding on the motorcycle from so far and entering the street where her house was at the end. Her heart suddenly started fluttering like a butterfly.

The postman put the letters in the letterboxes outside the homes; he came towards her house like stop and start.

It was her daily routine, she knew the timings when the postman arrived. She stood by the window early in the morning and waited for him. When he came, her heart fluttered like a butterfly and when he went without coming to her house, her heart came at the speed of a snail.

And at last today, her heart didn't need to go at the snail's pace from the fluttering butterfly. The postman was coming near to the letterbox of her house. She rushed downstairs.

"Is it my letter?" she said while coming towards him. He smiled and nodded his head in affirmation, taking out the letter from the bundle of letters, put it in her hand, and went ahead.

Before she would bend her eyes on the letter, her mother came and took that while saying,

"I am calling you incessantly so that you serve me a helping hand in making breakfast, and after even knowing it already that your dad needs to go early today, you are standing here!"

"Mamma, it's my letter!" She protested and tried to take the letter from her while ignoring each word she had said like all she said was in double Dutch.

"How it could be yours!" Mamma was surprised. "It would be of your dad," she said while setting her eyes on the letter, "See, it's your dad's."

Her heart was drowning, her breath stopped She bowed her head and went upstairs to her room.

In that heartache, the sun won't shine, birdsong passes as if the melody can't glide through the air as it once did before.

"Do you want the tickets?" she listened to her mother's voice asking her about the tickets when she was on the stairs.

She collects the postal tickets from her childhood, but at that point, she had no interest in managing them.

Even today, she didn't receive her letter.

*****

She spent her day as she did usually—in waiting. She was lying in the prone position on her bed; the laptop was in front of her on the pillow. It was midnight; the darkness was almost absolute, only a smattering light of laptop screen was scattered there. Even the moon had waned to almost nothing.

Her silky black hair laid down her back like black ink of a tilted piece of parchment. Her one hand's palm was below her chin, and she was moving her fingers of the other hand on the touchpad. She was seeing the screen with deep rapt and was moving her finger as she used to. After a click, a tab opened. And suddenly, her moving finger stopped; her set eyes showed the contemplation firstly and then restlessness. She quickly pressed some buttons.

"Loading..."

In that same mode of restlessness, waiting for the next page to open, she tucked her silky black hair by her slender finger behind her ear so that they wouldn't progress to her eye over and over.

After a few seconds, the page loaded. She neared her face towards the screen, and her silky hair again fell on her face, but she was still.

She was reading that page continuously, and her big black eyes were becoming more significant with shock. Her whole existence had been sunk in uncertainty. It took millions of seconds for her to believe that what she was reading was valid. She sat quickly on her bed.

Her phone was on the nightstand. She picked that and made a call quickly. The pressed buttons were the only sound, a breaker of the midnight silence. She connected the earbuds and tucked them in her ears, the call was ringing.

"Hello, Mishal!" The receiver had received the phone. "Were you awaken? Your sweet sister Abeeha here," she giggled.

"After waking me up from my beloved sleep, you are asking,was I awaken! You could even come to my room and check whether I was asleep or not. What a beautiful dream I was seeing..." Mishal started telling her about the dream. Abeeha listened to her a bit and then interposed her with a laugh.

"Just leave everything, Mishal, and listen to the big news I am telling you," she was now twisting her silky black hairs as she did, "And I am sure you will not believe that."

"Are you playing a prank on me?" interrogated Mishal.

"No, dear, NO. Rather, do one thing. I am not telling you, you guess that," advised Abeeha.

She averted the laptop and placed the pillow behind her on the bed crown for the back support and straightened the legs while neglecting Mishal's guesses.

"No."

"Nope."

"So far from the answer."

"Nothing of that kind."

"Seriously, Mishal, you will never get my point. Alas," Abeeha said, "Now listen to me carefully."

"Do you remember we both had applied for BCS scholarship at Bournemouth University? You know what, Mishal, they have selected me."

On the other side, Mishal had shouted that loud that Abeeha's tympanic membrane was just going to burst. Abeeha turned the laptop towards her and saw the screen carefully again.

"I am telling you the truth, Mishal. Just 10 minutes before, at 2:30, I got the email. You should also check just right now. You too had applied, you would have also got the email!" Holding the phone in one hand, she was shutting off the laptop from the other.

"Yes, I have seen Bournemouth on the internet. It is a quiet, peaceful, and beautiful place and the cost of living is lower compared to the UK's bigger cities..." She was telling everything about Bournemouth so interestingly that she didn't even know when the call had been declined.

"Hello! Hello! Are you listening?" said Abeeha when no one responded from the other side for so long.

Abeeha pushed the power button on the right side of the mobile. The glowing screen appeared, but there was nothing like a call. She became angry when she opened the call logs and came to know that she was talking to herself for six minutes continuously. But the next moment, she became calm. Her happiness was everything that time and nothing there could beat that.

She was waiting for the letter as she had thought this big news would come by the postman's hands, but she was not that much right.

*****

The light was oddly bright, casting the seagulls into dark shadows against a sky of palest blue.

Slowly and reluctantly, she uncovered her face. She blinked, was closing her eyes, and blinked again. Streaks of sunlight penetrated the window and blinded her. She sat up, dragged her feet off the bed, and rubbed her knuckles onto her eyes. She stretched her arms above her head and yawned. She watched her legs dangle above the off-white polyester carpet.

It was the brightness of a new page in the summer sun— the kind that brought a smile even as she let her eyes rest a moment. It was the sort of brightness that kindled something beautiful within. And at the same time, it stirred a connection with nature around. One of those days, the soul was so vibrant that it began to merge with every living thing, radiating, resonating and elevating.

She twirled the door lock and opened the door to see Mishal coming towards her. She smiled gently.

"Abeeha, I didn't get any of the emails," she propelled the half-opened door and entered inside; her face was filled with sorrow.

"It's all fine, Mishal. It will come in one or two days, no need to worry. We had applied together; I have been selected, so you will definitely be."

"But my name is also not mentioned in the scholarship program list, which is outside the main office. I had gone there early in the morning and just came now."

"And mine?"

"Only your name was stated there."

"Oh!" She honestly was in deep sorrow.

"Mishal, Abeeha, come quickly. The breakfast is ready," mother called out for breakfast.

They both saw each other's faces and bellowed, "Coming."

*****

HEAVY FEET

"Why smoking pipes?"

"Because I hate the way the smoke chokes me, but I also love the way it intoxicates me."

She inhaled that grey stench, the odor that foretold of tar-infested lungs and her future deathbed. There was something rotten in her eyes as she took each drag.

They were sitting on the corner bench of the garden. Zaini had evoked Zayan's assistant for bringing the smoking pipes. And he had got that for her though Eliza neither smoked nor she was smoking.

They were gossiping, but deep down, Eliza was just speaking and Zaini was just listening quietly, taking puffs of pipe smoke. She was listening to everything, but she couldn't register her talks ahead of the ears in her brain. Her brain had her own problems, and sitting there while listening to Eliza and smoking pipes, she was thinking about the money she will need in the blood transplant of her dad.

"The stars look so cool!" Zayan muttered in Zaini's ear, standing at the back of her bench. "So, are u ready...for...proving yourself?"

She looked back, and all she could see was Zayan's literal. He smirked and she felt paralyzed. His presence seemed to buzz around her like a fly that she could never swat. Every word, movement, and breath he performed seemed to infuriate her to no end. All of her thoughts were in a mental traffic jam. Everything else was falling away. Every natural body movement wass on hold. She must force something that mimicked what she should be doing: a smile, a fist bump, or what?

"Yes, I am," she murmured, as she finally got the sense to answer.

"Okayy! Come with me then."

They heard the soft clicks of Zaini's heels hitting the marble floor till they reached the desired place.

Zayan switched on the lights of the room. The room was like a perfect magazine cover. The white curtains were linen, the kind of white that is untouched by hands and devoid of dust. The two antique couches stood on the opposite sides of each hand-woven rug in front of the ashen fireplace. The couches were cream but inlaid with fine green silk; leaves embroidered so delicately that they might have landed there in spring and just sunk in. But she knew they took hundreds of hours to sew.

He invited both of them to sit, and they sat. He also sat on the other couch, and everyone started seeing each other.

"So," Zaini break the silence first, making eye contact with him while saying, "I am not here to prove myself. I am just here to tell you I don't need anyone, I don't need money. I am enough for myself and for all my needs; I don't need a sordid man like you," she said straight—her eyes filled with confidence.

"Zaini!" in the mode full of shock, Eliza was just able to call out her name.

Eliza's eyes were trained on some invisible specter. Her heavy eyelids a fraction too slow to blink, her irises too stationary, she became just numb.

On the other hand, staring had become his only form of link with her head. It was like her head was transparent, and he was fascinated by an object two inches behind her skull.

"Hahaha!" he finally got the senses to express something new. "Are you sure you don't need me or my money anymore?"

"Yes, I don't need you nor your money," said Zaini stridently. She was going towards the door at a rushing speed. He came and grabbed her arm.

"So why had you come here if you didn't need a sordid man like me? The place where you came is full of dirt. And if you came here, you need to accept that you are also sleazy with a sordid man in a dirty place," he kept saying. Zaini was becoming enraged. She was making unsuccessful efforts in letting her arm free. And a shake with her real power convulsed his whole body; he quivered backward.

"I came here to get a job, not for selling my honor, my respect, and my own worth. I wish I knew it first what kind of man you are so that I wouldn't have seen your face," said Zaini and went outside at a pretty damn fast speed.

*****

Face wiped clean as if a screen had been pulled down to hide her emotions, she hurried along. Fear sat heavily on her heart as she walked as fast as she could. Eyes plastered to the floor, she stared at her shoes. The cold painted bright red on her cheeks, and the wind threw her hair around aimlessly.

Walking across the tragic mess

Mossy trees and flowers less.

And she walked. She walked as her hair fluttered in the air, her clothes clung to her body, and arms tightly wrapped around her. She felt cold wind stroking her skin, wanting to rip her clothes off as if it were its enemy. A few teardrops appeared in the corners of her eyes, but Zaini continued walking, not stopping for anything.

"I wonder if I can breathe beneath the concrete. Part of me hopes for some day when these paths are more akin to a beautiful land, something natural that changes as the seasons do—something living," walking on the pavement, she was whispering to herself.

"Hello," an unknown man waved at her.

"Hello," she replied absent-mindedly.

"When did it become so insignificant? One word used to be a basis for communication. One word could create or break relationships, and now...It's become nothing more than an acknowledgment of existence. 'Hello,' to the old man passing on the street on our way home, never to be seen again, never again recognized as a person of significance. 'Hello,' we say, moving past the woman at the door. And that's it. Tell me what else do we say?" she asked herself. "No one bothers to say anything of meaning anymore. We're stuck in an endless loop, oblivious to the importance of people. They're just tools in our pointless existence, a way for us to try and convince ourselves of our own importance. We put on a mask of false friendliness, fake a smile and feign meaningful conversation, and then move on, forgetting that the other person was anyone of value," she told herself. "Well, wasn't that a depressing stream of thought?" she asked herself again—talking to her own self insanely.

"Hello," she waved to an unknown woman passing by her side, aware of the hypocrisy, and then moved on.

"Zzzz"

Zzzzz..."

The buzzer of her mobile phone went off like an annoyed rattlesnake. Zaini nervously pulled her phone out of her pocket and looked down at the phone's screen. Abeeha's name displayed; she answered quickly.

"Hello?"

"Hello, Ma'am! It's Abeeha. How are you?"

"Fine, what about you?"

"I am so happy, and I want to tell you a thing. Are you ready? May I tell you?" she felt giddy with excitement. She wanted to run, to shout, to tell everyone that the thing she was waiting for so long to happen has happened...but she had to wait. She couldn't read a book anymore, couldn't even manage her social media accounts. Her mind was like a butterfly. Whatever distraction she chose for herself, her mind kept fluttering back to the page of the laptop screen. Then she'd get that tingly feeling all over again.

"Yes, of course, Dear."

"Okayy! So...You know what, I had applied for a BCS scholarship at Bournemouth University. And you know, Ma'am, they have selected me, and I am so happy."

"Oh, wow! Looks like my kiddo has grown up," Zaini also became happy for her student and was becoming anxious to see her child, the one who had grown up too fast. A student's success can only make a teacher's mood happy when everything seems black to her. "Where is it? When will you depart?" asked Zaini while strolling on the pavement.

"It is a public university in Bournemouth, Dorset, England, and I need to leave on the 19th of April."

"Oh, that means you just have a week. Have you got your passport and visa?"

"Emm, I have traveled before, so I already have a passport. And I need to go to the British Embassy to apply for visa."

"Haven't applied for a visa yet! Why?" Zaini was shocked as she thought that she would have got the visa by now.

"Actually, everyone is busy at home, and I am scared to go alone. I don't know what the process will be there."

"Oh! I will come with you, no problem."

"Seriously!" she hadn't expected this kind of answer from the other side.

"Yes. We will meet at Allama Iqbal Library at 7:30 from where we will go to the British Embassy together and will reach there in the morning at sharp 8:00, right!" Zaini told her the whole program and solved her problem within a second. Her teacher was the only being to her that solved her problems in a snap.

"Okay, Ma'am, thank you so much. I am so happy, as happy as a kitty in a cream pie," she stayed carefree. Happiness had come looking for her itself.

"I am also happy, My Dear, as happy as a hippo in the mud," related Zaini and giggled. Abeeha giggled in return.

"So, enjoy your day, Dear. See you tomorrow."

"Okay, Ma'am, see you tomorrow, bye."

"Bye."

She looked down, declined the call, and put the phone in the pocket. She was truly happy for her student's success.

Happiness is like a radio signal that is loud one moment then gone the next. It is not always accompanied by laughter although laughter is good. Happiness is, most of the time, unpredictable. It often is a complete surprise. Happiness may last for a long while or it may pelt us with brief flashes. We could feel it at the unexpected sight of a loved one or at the brilliant sunset over the trees in the late evening. We may seek happiness, but it usually is an offshoot. Happiness usually happens as we take action and we are on the wing. We always open the door for joy, even for a brief moment. When we are low, that brief moment of pleasure can create an emotional mountain of relief.

*****

"All day long, I have been sitting at this desk, paperwork piling higher and higher. Gathering everyone's skills and taking out the top three, huh? The clock ticks on the wall, and I swear it's slowing down. Sitting here makes me flatter than a week-old glass of coke. Every time I don't have to think about the task at hand, I think of dance and dancing, dancing in the club to music so loud that it makes me deaf. With that music, that beat, those crazy, crazy lights tell me I'm alive, I'm real, and reality is awesome," she was gossiping with one of the employees.

The evening was as old as the coffee on the desk, waiting for someone to drink it.

She was in her office, piling up the files and getting ready for home, when the door began to bang, and a voice rose. They both saw each other and barely blinked. She just picked up her bag, her phone and walked towards the door.

Soon enough, they heard a door open, its creaking noise bringing a chill to her spine. It sounded like some dying animal, crying out its pain and sorrow with its last breath.

"Where?" he asked while staring at her as she turned herself into an everyday look from a personal secretary.

"Home," she had answered in the same manner as she got the question. Short.

"Before going home, come with me. I have something to show you," he ordered her straight.

"For me. To show. Sounds strange!" said Eliza, surprised.

"Follow me," he became swanky as the bosses commonly became and ignored what she said.

She started walking, walking unusually slowly, almost robotically, as if her brain was struggling to tell each foot to take the next step. It was as if she were in a stupor, like someone under hypnosis in one of those Scooby-Doo cartoons.

After a couple of minutes of walk, they reached a place where there was nothing but a single room. He opened the door and invited her to come with him inside.

The room floor denoted the highly polished wood, dark and free of either dust or clutter. Eliza eyed the coffee table. It was old-fashioned and mahogany, not one of those mass-produced items but real wood right the way through. She shuddered at the thought of what it cost to make, not in money but an old growth forest. A cursory look to the right showed her the almost hidden cords. There was no bookshelf, no dining table, only the chairs arranged around the fireplace filled with ashes. The photographs were black and white, not casual family snaps but looked as such by a professional.

"Sit, or after seeing what I have to show you, you will fall with shock yourself," said Sir Zayan with irony.

She sat so stiffly and with such a straight back that she gave off the impression of being a particularly strict schoolmistress. She pulled back her hair severely into a tight and twisted bun. He sat beside her, took out his smartphone from his jeans pocket, and started moving his fingers on the screen.

"Have you seen this girl? Who is she?" he asked in a sarcastic tone, uplifting one of his eyebrows and waiting for her to answer. She was just staring at the paused video of a dancing girl, of her best of the best friends, of Zaini!

"What is this? From where did you get this?" asked Eliza nervously.

"Don't worry, Dear, don't worry! I won't do anything till...Till you call your sweet friend and tell her to work in my academy or else...I could make this video viral, and then what the world calls her will not be my fault," he completed his sentence while giving a sarcastic smile.

"But..." she tried to argue.

"Calling or not?" he interposed.

"Okay!" she gave up.

Eliza's mind was starting to fail like an engine that turns over and over, never kicking into action. She couldn't formulate a thought. Every step could lead to more pain, and there was no way except calling her.

*****

Zaini looked upon his withered dad and king. He grew more wrinkled with each day, looking as though he had too much skin to cover his wilting frame. His face had lost its healthy brown color, fading to an ashy grey, looking as the dust had begun to gather on his rotting body. She remembered when her dad looked like a powerful man when he had hair and a beard so long that he could not tell where one ended and the next began. Now though, the king had lost his youthful and handsome looks. He was clean-shaven, and his hair was trimmed short, revealing a decrepit mask where every wrinkled, blemish, and imperfection could be seen.

Zaini was hurt when she looked at her father in this condition. She wished to remember the mountainous man he had been—the strong-willed and merciful king, the gentle and caring dad. Yet, when she looked upon him now, all she could see was a wizened and frightened old man. As she looked upon him, she wondered if her father was more scared of living or dying.

She sat crossed-legged on her dad's bed. All she wanted was for her dad to be well again. She was tired of his illness. She could hear his coughs from far beyond the walls of his house. She just wanted him to play with her as he used to play before.

"Zany!" a soft and calming voice came, which was enough for soothing her heart. Maybe he woke up.

"Yes, Dad!" she answered to her number one supporter, her gem, and her hero.

"Where had you gone? I thought you would be with Eliza."

Silence gnawed at her insides. It hung in the air like the suspended moment before a falling glass shattered on the ground.

"Yes, I was with Eliza," she answered him honestly.

"Was there any emergency? Because Eliza never comes so early," Dad had read his child's face.

"No, not emergency. She just gave me a surprise, and then I spent my day at Eliza's workplace,"

"Oh, that's good," he responded.

She didn't want dad to know about the diddlysquat stuff she gone through that day, but he was not comfortable with her answer. Although he reacted to agree, deep down, he didn't. But neither he said anything nor she told.

"Zzzz"

Zzzzz..."

Her phone buzzed. She pulled her phone out of her pocket and looked down at it.

"Who's calling?" asked Dad as she had become paused after seeing the phone's screen.

"It's Eli…za..." stuttered Zaini.

"So, answer her, Dear. What are you waiting for?" Dad continued.

"Yes..."

She stood up and, unfortunately, stumbled at the bed's bottom slide rail. She didn't even stop to see her foot to see if it's fair, bleeding or not. But she didn't and went towards the window as she was making herself strong enough to listen to something dreadful. To listen to something unexpected.

"Hello, Zaini?" came a voice from another side with quite an uneasiness.

"Yes, Eliza," she tried to sound natural though her heart was accelerating at full speed.

"Zaini! Can you tell me a thing true?" asked Eliza tensely.

"Are you okay, Eliza? What happened?" She was surrounded by overwhelming feelings of anxiety.

"I am okay, Zaini. Please, will you tell me a thing true?"

"But what's the matter? Where are you?" she was dismayed.

"I am at a place where you left me all alone. Why don't you tell me?" she sobbed. "Will you answer my question truly?"

"Yes!" answered Zaini nervously.

Have you ever sent Angela's birthday party video to Sir Zayan? Do you know him already?"

There was absolute stillness. No air stirred the grass or leaves. No clouds drifted in the sea of blue above. No water dripped or flowed. Not a sound could be heard either close at hand or in the far off distance. Even her own breath seemed to die as soon as it left her mouth.

"No," she hadn't expected this kinda question.

"But he has shown me."

"But trust me, I haven't sent him any of the videos," she became husky.

"Do you know what people could do with that? Do you ever wonder, Zaini?" she burst out.

"Eliza, it was not me, trust me."

"Okay, I trust you," she took a breath, "But listen to me, I know you are not that kinda girl. I know you couldn't do such types of things, I trust you." she became calm. "But the world doesn't; you need to protect yourself from the world's evil eyes."

"Eliza! Can you tell me directly what's going on there?" she had become scared.

"Zaini! Don't worry, this all gonna be okay."

"But, please tell me, what's the matter?"

"Sir Zayan got that video, and he is saying if you do not work with him, he will make that video viral."

"Eliza!" she became unable to speak further.

"Don't worry, Zaini, I am with you. Come right now, and we will solve this matter so soon."

"Are you sure I should come?!"

"Zaini, your respect matters; you need to come."

In that mysterious darkness, the deep face was far more than just the absence of light.

"Okay, I am coming in an hour," she said tiredly.

"Don't worry, Zaini, everything will be fine," she supported her.

"Yes," said Zaini shortly.

She removed the phone from the ear, looked down, declined the call, and sighed. The sigh that escaped Zaini's dry lips was slow as if her brain needed that time to process what had happened. Her eyes remained fixed on the scary sky outside the window.

The darkness fell with darkey clouds.

She has been wrapped with mystery shrouds.

Night had fallen fast upon the land. No more than an hour ago, the sky was painted with hues of red, orange, and pink. But all color had faded, leaving only a matt black canvas with no stars to be looked upon. The darkness was thick.

Other than the darkness and herself, all that seemed to exist was the chilly wind whose harsh bite could be felt through her clothes. She could feel the hairs on her arms, the sharpness of wind that left its mark in the form of small bumps that were tingling on her arms. Her blood ran cold through her veins, and her bones were chilled.

"Is this a punishment of any of my sin?" she asked herself.

*****

Her head throbbed. The pain felt like someone had taken a knife to her skull as she leaned her head against the window. Squeezing her eyes shut, she willed the pain to go away. The rest of the world became detached; all she could concentrate on was the pain rooted deep in her head. All she felt, all she knew, was the pain of that moment.

In a few moments, she realized that she wasn't alone in the room. Dad was still with her. She decided to tell him the truth as she thought that the truth never hides. It will definitely reveal itself. 'It would be better to tell the truth, right now,' she thought.

She stumbled to the corner of the room. And with each step, her stomach tightened and ached all the more. She kept swallowing, and her throat kept clenching, but no matter what, she could not stop the warm feeling rising through her chest.

She sat crossed-legged beside Dad. He was looking the same as he used to. Sick. His hands were debilitated and greyish. Face covered with dark circles, black lips, swelled eyes, and pale yellow color.

"What happened? Is she okay?" he asked with care.

'Yes, Dad, she is fine. Everything is fine," in the process of swallowing tons of tears, she lied. She was unable to tell him the truth after focusing on his health.

"So, why did she call you?" asked Dad as he was in doubt.

"She wants me to have dinner with her. May I go, Dad?" And again, a lie slipped off her tongue. She asked for permission as she knew that Dad will never say no to her.

"For dinner! Yes, you may go," he gave the permission.

"Okay, I am taking a bath right now. Then I will go. Do you need anything?" she asked.

"No, Dear, just enjoy your dinner."

"Yes, Dad," she could only say yes as millions of pieces of her soul had torn off.

She stepped into the shower, toes flinching as they touched the chilled ceramic floor. Her mind was in shreds; she was unable to control her head. She turned the tap, old and metallic, releasing thousands of lukewarm drops darkening her hair and trickling down her back. Her eyes closed over and over, and each time, they showed that corrupt face.

As she came out, her eyes were enough to tell that she had been crying for a long time. Her watery eyes looked as if an ocean had been encased.

Zaini hadn't given attention to herself. She had an idea of how she would be looking. So, instead of looking at herself in the mirror and putting on some makeup, she took out the coat, which was a gift from her father, and put it on. It was still looking new though it was many years old. She never wore it. She thought that only odd and low-class people wore it, but now she got to know the worth of that coat.

"Dad, I am going. Do you need anything?" she called out while standing at the door.

"No, Dear. You may go but return early. Goodbye," he replied.

"Yes, Dad! Take care, Goodbye," she responded and stepped out.

Soon, it began sprinkling—little droplets of water -drenched Zaini's hair, skin, and dress. The water droplets began growing larger and falling frequently, and the rain started on the way to getting an auto.

Kissed by the rain and glistening, the wet ground was cold underfoot. Walking on the path, Zaini felt the squelch of the mud beneath. The water rose up and ran between her toes. She would take an auto, but the rain fell softly as if it knew of the hardships both behind and ahead. It takes a time of quiet safety for the child-self to reemerge into the consciousness and have the courage to pull up a chair at the self's elegant table. Walking in the rain became a perfect time to gain that sense of safety, of inner peace, and the courage to listen to what the child-self had to say.

But let her see the baby rain.

Forming its path in thorny ways.

There is a serenity in the rain, a sense of peace that offers to resonate with the soul's peaceful elements. Walking among those drops was her meditation, a way to fully become present at the moment, a way to feel free.

Something about a rain-washed pathway invites playful feet, which says each new step will be rewarded with a splash.

The academy was not near her house, but the calming walk of an hour was far more beautiful than 15 minutes of the auto ride. She was unaware of her swollen feet, which was the result of a continuous hour-long walk. But each raindrop is a doorway into nature's heart. She wanted to enjoy that.

*****

"Boo!" yelled Zaini to frighten her while standing at the back of the garden bench where she was sitting.

"Who?!" squealed Eliza. She became so scared that her heart forgot to beat.

"Hahaha, calm down; it's me."

"Huff, you frightened me so much that I jumped out of my."

"Awww, you are still a lil baby," she scoffed.

"You are!"

"Okay, okay, leave it, Lil Baby," mocked Zaini.

"Hmm," she didn't give any sort of remarkable response.

"So...What's the matter?" She sat beside and asked her in a solemn mood, but she was calming herself, deep down.

"I'm gonna tell you, but you need to listen first to whatever I say, then speak, okay!"

"Okay."

"So...Sir Zayan has your video, and he wants you to work with him, or else he will make that viral. My advice to you is to work with him..."

"Never, I..."

"Lemme speak first," Disrupted Eliza.

"My advice to you is to work with him; he will pay high. I am just saying this for your good. Now you are permitted to speak."

"Firstly, the question arises why he wants me to work with him. He could get anyone, I am not the only and lonely girl left on this universe. Secondly, who am I to him? We are not long-term enemies, so why would he harm me? Who the hell is he?" she became whacked.

"You will get your answer," a voice came from somewhere. They both started seeing near and far till they found Zayan walking towards them. "You will get your answer, don't worry, Lollipop," he said, standing in front of them.

"What do you want? What wrong I have done to you?" shrilled Zaini.

"I am helping you."

"What kinda help? Why are you helping me?"

"I have been waiting for today for a long time."

"But why?!" she pierced.

"You will get your answer, but for that, you need to work with me."

"Or if I don't."

"You better know the consequence."

"Fuck you."

"Thank you."

A long silence held between them. The silence was the most terrifying part—like before a bomb, before the explosion.

"So...Will you work with me or else...?" he left his sentence incomplete and waited for the answer.

"But why do I work with you?" questioned Zaini.

"Working or not," he became vulgar.

"I want my answer, Goddammit!" she said raucously.

"Working with me serves many favors, and refusing my work destroys a person," he said arrogantly.

"Okay, but only work, not anything else," she agreed after a minute of silence, "and you will pay me much high."

"Your order, most willingly, Buttercup," he said while bowing to her. "Anything else?"

"No," she said while directing towards the gate to go.

"Going from now? Don't want to talk with me...about...the work?"

"No!" she said straight and started taking steps to go. "And," she said while looking back and pointing at Zayan, " If you ever wanted to talk with me, FIRST call me to take the time and then start your tosh. 'Cos I don't have enough time especially for YOU, or you may say it's all about priorities."

"Okayy, Madam," said Zayan

Instead of listening to his affirmation, she went. She had an extreme headache, and she just needed rest.

She reached home in an auto and peeked in her dad's room to see whether he was sleeping or not. She breathed deep and thanked God that he was asleep; she didn't need to lie this time. She went into her room upstairs and lay on her bed directly.

Her mind screamed out as the pain drove through her back. The burning pain licked up her back like a scorching fire. She wept at her own suffering. She rolled up in a ball of self-loathing and despair, wishing the world to end. The sea of constant currents, some strong, some weak, but the waves always crashed over her, permanently.

Or is there something hidden in that pain? Maybe she would know it further. Or maybe not.

*****

WITH PAIN COMES THE TRUTH

"Lookin' fly F-f-flossin'"

"Lookin' fly F-f-flossin'"

"Lookin' fly F-f-flossin'...."

Her phone rang and kept ringing until she woke up and declined it. She incidentally had turned off the vibrating mode of her mobile last night. It was 7 o'clock. She forgot to set her alarm to wake up, as she had to meet Abeeha at sharp 7:30.

"Hello, Ma'am! It's Abeeha. Were you sleeping?"

"Yes, Kid. I was tired last night, so I forgot to set the alarm."

"Oh, so sorry, you may take some rest. We will go tomorrow, no problem," replied Abeeha.

"No, Dear, I am fine now. You are worthy of a thank you as your call woke me up," said Zaini," I will reach the library at 7:30. You may also get there," she added.

"Okay, Ma'am, see you in 30 minutes. Thanks for your cooperation. Bye."

"Bye," ended Zaini.

She brushed her teeth, washed her face, changed her clothes, and made breakfast for dad. She did all this work in just 20 minutes. She left a coupon and a note on the door of her dad's room that said:

"I AM GOING WITH ABEEHA TO APPLY FOR HER VISA, AS SHE GOT SCHOLARSHIP IN AN ENGLAND UNIVERSITY. BREAKFAST IS READY, AND THE COUPON FOR LUNCH AND DINNER IS ON THE DINING TABLE. I WILL TRY TO COME BACK EARLIER. BUT I DON'T KNOW THE EXACT TIME, SO I HAVE LEFT THE PREPARED BASIC ESSENTIALS FOR YOU. IF YOU NEED ANYTHING, YOU COULD, AND YOU SHOULD CALL ME. OKAY, DAD. TAKE CARE.

REGARDS,

YOUR CHEETOS."

She stepped outside the house, looked at the sky, took a deep breath, and relaxed. She knew it was a new day with a beautiful atmosphere with no thunderstorm, and there will definitely be opportunities to rebuild herself. She was her dad's supergirl that never gives up, and YES, she will never give up.

"Stop here, please," she told the auto uncle to stop at the Allama Iqbal Library gate where Abeeha was already standing.

"Hello, Ma'am," spoke Abeeha when she saw Zaini coming towards her.

"Hello, Kid." They both shook hands and greeted each other. They took an auto for the British Embassy. The jammed traffic, the horn noises, closed signals, and snared cars were all the same as they used to. She was frequently seeing her wristwatch and then the slow-moving traffic. They finally reached there at 8:03 am, but they had a wonderful conversation in this duration, and it surely meant a lot for both of them.

After some standard checking, they finally reached a big hall where they were meant to sit and wait for their turn. The ceiling of the chamber must be twenty-feet high. Designs of fruit and flowers were carved into the molding. Cloying scents were coming from the vases of blossoms that made their eyes itch.

"You have been called inside," announced a strange man who came to them when they had just sat on the chairs.

A good-looking man was waiting for them. Walking behind her teacher, she was nervous. Zaini took the documents from Abeeha and gave them to the men sitting on the mirror window's other side. Abeeha's heart was beating fast. What if her visa got rejected?

The officer took the file from Zaini, took out the forms, and put the file back. If he wanted to give the visa, he would take the interview, ask some questions, and check the documents. But he just took a cursory look over the form and saw both of them with demureness. Abeeha felt suffocated; she was not even able to blink her eyes.

"Where were you? I am waiting for you for many days," asked the man and picked up a paper from a table next to him. "Bournemouth University has sent me this list. Your name is mentioned here, which means I need to put up your visa. Anyways, your visa will come tomorrow. You may receive it from here in the evening, right?"

"Right," said Zaini.

Abeeha was unable to speak. It looked like her voice was trapped in her voice box. The heart was beating so fast that it was just going to come out of her chest. As soon as they came out, they both stared at each other.

"My Dear, best of luck with your journey," said Zaini.

Abeeha didn't speak a word. Zaini walked up to her slowly and squeezed her cheeks. The world around her melted away. She had admitted that she was going to England to study, for doing BCS, which was all unbelievable for her.

"I will be a topper. Will you feel proud?" questioned Abeeha with innocence.

"Yes, Kiddo, of course," answered Zaini softly.

But has anyone seen the future? Will Abeeha even go to England? Who knows!

*****

"Isn't it's so early to go back home?" asked Abeeha with a little puckishness.

"Hahaha, well, you are right," spoke Zaini, "So, where should we go now?"

"Emm...There," said Abeeha while pointing at the clothes outlet.

"Nice idea, there is a flat 70% off on all items. We should buy something before the boost in prices," said Zaini with the same impishness.

They just crossed the road and reached the outlet. Zaini and Abeeha both entered by thrusting the glass door inside.

The crowd was definite. There was a mixture of the air conditioner's coolness and the heatstroke-heat coming from outside as the door was frequently opening. The outlet was sparkling by the overdone lighting. The clothes, especially the embroidered ones, were placed and hanged everywhere, and the people were buzzing around the clothes like the honey bees on the beehives.

Zaini and Abeeha were sauntering, looking at the dummies' clothing and the dresses placed on racks and shelves. Behind the cash counter, a salesman was standing. As he looked at them, he promptly came nearer to them, became attentive, and asked:

"Yes, ma'am, may I help you?"

"Show me that pearl white dress with cherry red-colored embroidery," said Zaini while pointing at the dress placed on the unstitched clothes corner in the wooden rack.

"Ma'am, I have already taken it out; there it is," he was pointing a few feet far from her where a man and woman were standing, inspecting that cloth.

"Oh, thanks," she first saw that unstitched dress in their hands and then saw that couple.

"We must buy it. I will wear it at the upcoming event. Will I look prettier in it?" the woman was convincinging the man, and Zaini was just seeing them, unable to look somewhere else.

"Let's go from here, Abeeha," said Zaini rapidly; her heart was broken off.

"Okay, Ma'am," She agreed as she had noticed Zaini's changing mood.

*****

The midnight had fallen like a rich velvet blanket of black, swallowing up the day, draining the colors to grey and then to nothing at all.

She had dropped Abeeha at her home and spent the rest of the day locked in her bedroom. She had just come out to look after dad twice or thrice, and her mobile was switched off the whole day.

The pain she was going through wasn't sharp like needlepoint or a knife. It was burning around her innards. Everything felt scolded to her; she was in more pain than she could have ever imagined was possible. A bullet would be a mercy to her, but the morphine with a higher dose was the best she could hope for.

While lying on the bed with the feeling of sickness in the middle of the night, she heard a very low noise of a door opening and the door closing.

"Who would it be at this time?" queried Zaini to herself.

She stood up, opened the room's door, and started taking steps at a low pace. As soon as she got to know who was on the door and now who wass in the bathroom, the pain turned into anger. Anger boiled deep in her system, as hot as lava. She knew it's too much for her to handle. The pressure of that raging sea of anger would force her to say things she did not mean or express thoughts she had been suppressing.

"Where were you?" she asked as soon as she got out of the bathroom.

"I was at your aunt's house!" she let herself look comfortable though the liars could never be comfortable with their lies.

"Are you sure?" inquired Zaini with confidence.

"So, what's so futuristic in that?"

"You are lying," said Zaini assuredly.

"Are you in your senses? I am your mother; don't you have any manners?" said mother angrily.

"No, neither I am in my senses nor I have any manners because my mother never taught me," she burst out.

"Don't you dare to say that again, understand? You have lost all your senses," she said sharply.

"No, today, I will not become silent. Today, you need to answer all my questions," her anger was boiling up.

"Zaini, shut up and go to sleep."

"No, tell me, where were you? I haven't seen you at home for many days. Where were you, Mother? Where were you?" she asked raucously.

"I have told you I was at your aunt's house. I am your mother; don't act like you are. So, cut the crap now and get off," she yelled.

"If you were at my aunt's house, who was at the outlet with Zayan?" she had finally asked the real question.

This question made her mother astounded like the ground beneath her feet slipped away. A wave of questions was coming continuously into her brain. How did she see me? How did she know about Zayan? Did she know everything?

She came towards her and slapped her hard just because her sin had been caught, and she couldn't bear this insult. She didn't want Zaini to spill out more. She inflicted her anger on her daughter. The slap was as loud as a clap and stung her face. It had been an open-handed smack, and had left a red welt behind. Just below her eye, skin had been scraped off by the ring mother was wearing. She staggered backward, clutching her face, eyes watering.

"You can't be my mother," she shouted while running back to her room.

*****

THE BEGINNING OF THE REAL JOURNEY

She woke up by a message ringtone. She had slept last night crying and sobbing on her bed. She opened the mobile phone to check whose message it was. As soon as she opened the phone, she got to know it wasn't a usual message. It was an email; she was shocked as she hasn't expected email these days. She opened that email straight away, and it gave her another shocking news. Zayan had emailed her the ticket of PIA. It was for 19 April from Pakistan to India.

Her phone vibrated, and now it was a text message from Zayan that said:

"HOPE YOU GOT THE TICKET. YOU NEED TO PRINT IT OUT. YOU WILL DEPART FROM PAKISTAN FOR INDIA. WE WILL HAVE THE REST OF THE CONVERSATION WHEN YOU WANT. THANK YOU."

Red-hot tears ran down her face. Her loose shoulders shook, Her hands hanging low, she made no attempt to conceal or even wipe away her own tears. Aside from her reddened face, she was so grey looking, and her hair was as disheveled as the park under fall leaves. It was how people cry when they lose their children. It's a kind of crying that shows that the hurt has cut right back through the protective layers acquired in maturity.

Dad was staring at the walls, downstairs in the bedroom, his face creased, and his fists closed so tight he could feel the sweat trapped inside them. That's when he heard a sound that almost stopped his heart. Just above his room, he heard a sobbing sound, like a small child who'd lost her mother. But there was no small child in the room, only her daughter. He turned to go upstairs, hands grasping the rail, shoulders shaking, and the sound of struggling to breathe against the crying.

"Zany!" he called when he opened her room's door and saw the weird situation inside.

There was no response other than an intensification of the grief.

"Kid, what have you done to yourself?" he said while placing his hand on her shoulder.

She didn't respond, but her dad didn't leave her. He kept sitting there. His sitting was something that told her she was not alone; someone was still there to hold her when her own existence was at a loss of lifting up herself.

After some countless minutes, she saw in her dad's eyes lovingly and said;

"Dad, I love you a lot. Please don't ever leave me alone."

"My honey, don't worry, I am with you, and I love you too," he replied with affection.

"But, Dad, I am your deceitful child," she said sorrowfully.

"Oh no, Honey, what are you saying! You are my love, and I am sure I am yours."

"Yes, Dad, you are," she sighed, "but I will leave you. I am deceitful. Admit it," she said with a trembling voice.

"Why are you saying so?" he inquired.

"I am leaving you, this country on 19 April," said Zaini and breathed, "I got a job of the director of neoclassical ballet in an academy in India."

"But, Zaini." he said with a quivering voice.

"Sorry, Daddy, I didn't tell you earlier."

"When will you return?" he was unable to say anything else.

"So soon, Dad, so soon."

Dad didn't say anything. He pulled her closer and wrapped her in his arms. It was a hug, a hug of gentle arms that gives her space to breathe. It was a hug of strong arms that tell everything she is and a beautiful sense that he is with her. She loved both the duvet and the human shield, but he was crying. Zaini had never seen her superhero, her superman, her love, and her dad crying in her life—crying so bitterly as a child cries when he cannot tell someone how much the wound hurts.

"Dad, I am really sorry," she felt guilty. She had made her daddy cry.

"No problem, Honey, you are my ballerina. I am so proud of you," he said and kissed her forehead.

They both exchanged smiles. They both had remembered days when there was no reason to smile—when everyone led their most nuanced lives, and the lives were in full swing.

*****

The building was standing with its brilliant luster and splendor. AC chilled the office. Zayan was sitting reclining his back on the comfy chair behind the bossy table, staring at the lady, Zaini's mother, thoughtfully.

"How did she know about you?" she was asking angrily.

"She came to me for a job, and I have hired her," he replied.

"How could you do that? Why didn't you tell me? You knew she is my step-daughter."

"She was just a normal girl for me. I meet thousands of girls and thousands of people every day. Do I need to tell you of everyone?" he explained.

"Now boot her out," she ordered

"I can't. I have given her the ticket for 19 April for India."

"How can you be so much hasty?" she became sarcastic.

"I am not hasty. It's my work, and I know what to do," he answered, "Why don't you tell her about us," he asked caustically.

"It's my matter, not yours," she answered straight, "If you couldn't boot her out, then kill her."

"Kill her!" he was surprised. "She is your daughter. Are you insane?"

"Why are you so amazed? Haven't you ruined other's lives before? Now, do it this time again!" she said comfortably.

"Haha! You have also become evil-minded. But here in this situation, the killing will not be the solution," he told her.

"Why? It's the easiest way to cut her off."

"I don't want you to be in the red zone; killing her is risky."

She sneered and stood by the window to look outside. Enrobed in a long black gown and shiny pearl jewelry, she was looking sad and agitated.

"Why are you worrying? Zayan will manage everything," he said with calm.

*****

"Welcome back! I've been waiting for this day for so long," said Dad with pure love, sitting on the dining table in the faded t-shirt.

"We are having dinner together after a long time," said Zaini.

Dinner with Dad was always like a rock 'n' roll party. No restrictions like elbows off the table, sitting up straight, chewing with mouth shut, taking small bites, making pleasant conversation, not talking with a full mouth, finishing the plates, using a napkin, asking permission to leave the table, helping clear the table, sweeping the floor and washing the dishes. Dinner with Dad was always relaxed. In front of the telly, laughing at the comedy show, dropping beans all over the room, talking with mouth full of toast, spraying crumbs over the carpet, drinking from glass perched precariously, piling plates on the counter next to the dishwasher, as they both sat, laughing unpleasantly on the comedy show and the jest they were sharing.

"What have you done with your hair? They are so thin now." interrogated Dad softly.

"Oh, Dad, I have done nothing. It's just your caring eyes," she replied smoothly.

"After a long time, my room is lit up, or you just lit up my room. I was feeling like I was a dark day under a dense cloud sheet, but now it doesn't even matter. I have a ray of God-given sunshine at my table. Radiant, My Dear, you are radiant," he said lovingly.

"Dad, it's all your love!" answered Zaini. "May I ask you a thing if you don't mind?"

"Yes, sure, Kid."

"Why Mom never sits with us? I rarely see her at home," she asked.

"Did she say something to you ‘coz you never ask me this kinda question?”

"No, no, I am just asking."

"She has a lot of work to do. So, she usually doesn't come home," told Daddy, "Will you go somewhere tomorrow?" he tried to change the topic.

"Yes, Daddy, of course. I have much work to do before departing from here," she answered.

"Then go, take a refreshing sleep. May God bless you."

"But, Daddy, I wanted to ask a question," she protested.

"Yes, yes, My Dear, you may," he replied.

"Who we are, I mean from which religion we relate to?"

"How did you get this kinda thought?" he questioned curiously.

"I am just asking," she declared.

"You go right now; you would need some rest. We will talk about this some other day," he was commanding her.

"Okay, Dad, you may also have a refreshing sleep," agreed Zaini.

They both kissed each other, and she went to her room. She left the room, confused. Why didn't Dad answer me? And from that moment, she decided to decipher who she really was in terms of religion. That’s when her real journey began!

*****

To the left of her dad's bed where he was sleeping after taking the afternoon pills and was probably seeing the beautiful dreams, a wooden cabinet stood alone. Yet, it looked for all the world as if it belonged to a seafaring pirate and had spent decades in the free-spun salty air.

In the next afternoon of the memorable dinner, Zaini was sitting in front of the cabinet, finding some of the reports that were misplaced, medicines which she needed to buy, seeing appointment card to know when she would need to take Dad to the hospital for the checkup. She needed to wind up every sort of work before departing.

As soon as she opened the cabinet drawer, she found the crates of photographs. She picked up one of her childhood photos in which she was sitting beside her tall, young, powerful dad. She started seeing each picture one by one, flipping over each photograph. She felt she had reached some new world OR in some of the old, beautiful and cheerful world.

Those photographs were just conduits to her best memories, the ones that were not fantastic enough or traumatic enough to leave a permanent mark on their own.

"I need these memories to stay with me. I need them to soothe me when the bad ones threaten to erase all traces of those people I still hold dear, even in their absence. They are evidence of the beautiful souls that belong even to those who would have made the worst mistakes, ‘coz every being is allowed to make a mistake," she thought.

She stopped, stuck at two different pictures. The first picture was of her dad and a lady who seemed to her a little familiar, but Zaini could not comprehend who she actually was. That lady was with a one or two-month-old baby in her lap, and beside her was likely a giggling six-year-old child who was Zaini without any doubt. The second picture showed her dad with her wife or Zaini's disgusting mother, holding possibly an eight-year-old child's hand, of Zaini's hand. In that, her face was looking like a person leading a cumbersome life.

She was confused. She could see something hidden in those pictures but was unable to get it. She was questioning herself;

"Who is this second baby?"

“Who is this unknown lady?”

“Why is Dad with her?”

“Why am I with her?”

“Why am I so much happy in this unknown scenario?”

“Why am I looking drained with my own family?”

“At which point these pictures correspond?..."

She questioned herself a lot, but neither did she get the answers nor her confusion left her. She decided to ask Dad about those pictures, but neither could she nor Dad would answer.

"Now, what can I do? Why is our family so much mysterious?" she questioned herself again.

She kept staring at both pictures, focusing and pressurizing her mind so that she could remember something important that she might be forgetting, or so that she could reach a point where it would be easy to solve this maze. But she was unable to do anything.

And Boom! She got an idea, a very first step to solve this puzzle. She took out her mobile phone from the pocket and took explicit pictures of those two photographs. This will help her solve this maze without letting Dad know.

She went to her mother's room, which was locked. She opened the door like a spy with her hairpin and directly went to a cabinet beside the bed. It was clasped. Zaini tried to open it again by the hairpin, but she couldn't, so she started finding the key. “It would be in the bedroom,” she thought. She searched for the it and after tireless searching of half an hour, she found it inside the cushion cover.

She opened the cabinet and then the drawer. Yeah, there was what she had thought, a crate of pictures. She started finding those two photographs here also, but she had just seen the second one, not of the unknown lady. She also found many pictures of herself, her dad, her mother, and many of her mother and Zayan.

"Oh, hell! Where will this all end??" she thought as she was worn out after seeing many photographs of her mother and Zayan together.

She opened the mobile phone again and took two pictures, one of Zayan and mother and one of that photograph she had also found in Dad's cabinet's drawer. She decided to find out the analogous point of these pictures, and she was sure she would discover it.

On the way, an adventure to find who she really was and where she belonged. Who these people actually were and what kind of relationship she had with them—a real adventure, a whole journey.

*****

He was already sitting, waiting for her for an hour to talk with her about some necessary things before departing. And finally, she had come. He tried to greet her warmly, but he failed as Zaini was in an elevated mood.

"Congratulations!" he tried again to start a friendly conversation.

"Thank you," she replied.

"Let me show you something," he said and opened the table drawer. "Wait, please, I am searching for it... I don't know why

I couldn't find the right things at the right time," he was busy, finding. "Yes, here it is," he said while giving the envelope to Zaini, "It's your hotel booking voucher and visa. The ticket is already with you...Have you ever gone to India before?"

"No."

"That's also fine, don't worry! You just need to take the taxi and show him this voucher. He will see the address and will drop you there."

"Eliza will come with me, am I right?" she asked.

"No, but she will come a day after you reach there. That means your flight is of 19 April and hers is of 20 April."

"And why have you arranged our flights separately?" she inquired.

"It was a mistake done by the airport management; it's not my fault," he lied.

"Okay... May I go now?" Her work was done now. She just wanted to disassociate.

"Yes...May I drop you?" he asked with fake respect.

"Never," she refused with tediousness.

*****

"How is my shoogie-woogie?" he asked sweetly.

As soon as Zaini went out of his office, he ringed Zaini's mother, Alisha, to tell her his mischievous plan.

"Fine, have you done my work?" she asked directly without any ado.

"Yes."

"How?"

"You asked me to kill her, but do you know how to kill a person while keeping them alive?" he asked.

"Please, I am not in a mood to play these riddle games," she responded with annoyance.

"Okay, okay...I have got some of her information, and I got to know what kind of nature she has and at which level she hates or loves a person. So, the easiest way to kill her while keeping her alive is to kill or harm a person she loves!"

"Are you going to kill her dad? My husband!?" she asked curiously.

"No, I don't need to kill him; he is already dying," he laughed, "I will kill her best of the best friends Eliza, my personal secretary."

"And...How?"

"It's my headache; you don't need to worry, Sweety. Your work will be done in its perfect manner."

"Thank you so much, Zayan, you have solved half of the problem."

"My pleasure, Dear."

"I am so proud of your evil mind," she appreciated his work.

"You are also like those people who say I'm evil, but I say I'm just wired differently," he said reluctantly, "Tell me do you find a squirrel cute?" he asked.

"Yes, of course, squirrels are always cute," she answered.

"Hahaha, but I couldn't see any of the cuteness in them. Others like you look at a squirrel and see something cute, but I see something I can kill. I don't want to just shoot it though, I want to see how long it can last while I disembowel it nicely and slowly. I want to see the light go out in its rodent eyes while I examine its innards. I could say it's for science, but that would be a lie. The truth is I enjoy it. I get a kick out of it, and I'll record it on my phone, too, so I can play it over and over to relive the moment. Just be glad it's a squirrel in my sights right now; soon, I'll graduate to bigger and better things. In some human cultures, a guy like me would be valued for our skills; we'd be honored. Maybe I'll go abroad and be some kind of mercenary one day." He described her as a monster.

"I admire; you are just wired differently." She said, and they both giggled.

*****

THE FLIGHTS

Night, a silent charcoal curtain, had finally fallen, wrapping the day in its dark blanket. There was a strange stiffness in that night. The night was starless, and the moon was covered by murky clouds blended in the rest of the sky.

He was taking shelter under a tree after parking his car far from his existence. The electricity had gone off there, and the street was lying isolated. The lights of some houses were glowing sporadically by the grace of uninterruptible power supply, and the rest of the world was almost hidden by the darkness. Accordingly, a cap-wearing man couldn't be recognized from a distance. His eyes were evident of evil action.

It was the night of 18 April when Abeeha was sobbing at the door, hugging her mother and Mishal, and was just going to depart from her house for the airport.

She hired a taxi, which was of her dad's friend, sat inside, and perfectly put all her luggage. Her flight was at 6:00 am, but she had left her home at 3:00 am. According to the airport rule, passengers should arrive at the airport 2 hours before their flights, and she would need an hour to get there.

After a rushing drive of 55 minutes, she had reached the airport. She was moving towards the boarding area to complete her boarding when she thought to talk to Ma'am Zaini one last time before departing from Pakistan. She took out the phone and started walking to a silent place to converse comfortably. "But she would be sleeping," she thought. She texted her:

"I AM AT THE AIRPORT AS YOU KNOW I AM GOING TO BOURNEMOUTH UNIVERSITY, ENGLAND. I JUST WANNA SAY THANKS AND GOODBYE. I LOVE YOU AND WILL MISS YOU ALOT."

She texted and waited for the reply. She wanted to talk, but she couldn't wait more so she ringed Ma'am Zaini and placed the phone on her ear.

Ringing...

"Hello," the receiver had received the call.

"Hello, Ma'am, how are you? I am at the airport," told Abeeha.

"Oh, wow, at what time will you finally depart?" she asked.

"My departure is..." the phrase remained on her lips. Someone had pulled her phone mightily; she hadn't got a chance to look back or scream. Someone had put his hands on her mouth and pinched a needle-like sharp thing on her nape. It was an act of just a moment. Black clouds were coming in front of her eyes. Before her narcosis of the brain, the last thing she felt was someone was lugging her backward. And then, darkness surrounded her from everywhere.

"Hello."

"Hello..."

"Hello, Abeeha..."

"Abeeha..." she kept saying, but no one answered. She ended the call and thought that maybe the signals had dropped or there might be an emergency. She left a message of good regards and started doing her packing, as she also had to depart from

Pakistan for India at 9:00 pm. Busy in her work, she was unaware of what had happened.

*****

Her plane had successfully landed at the India airport. It was the only hopeful flight of 2 hours and 10 minutes—the hope of curing Dad and keeping him alive for a long time.

She took a taxi and went to the desired hotel. She was a confident and strong daughter of a superhero. She remembered her dad's saying:

"My daughter is an eagle. My daughter is a fish swimming upriver. My daughter is a young lioness on the prairies. I used to think of my daughter, you, as a flower waiting to bloom or a delicate spring leaf, but you are so much more. You have your own wings, your own propulsion, and your own inner strength. It isn't that you have shed your vulnerabilities. As a dad, I know where they all are, but you have your own future to strive toward. It's time for me to adapt, to no longer walk each path in front of you unless you ask me to. I am letting you travel alone, making sure you know your right way to walk on." He was saying this with tear-filled eyes when she was hugging him at the door one last time before going to the airport.

Her eyes watered by her dad's remembrance and his love, or by the happiness of her belief that now she would be able to get her dad cured and he will be that young man again one day.

*****

In the morning of the next day, the people sitting on the other side of the table were whispering.

"You need to become the best director," two of the ladies stated.

Zaini was listening to them and was thinking of her dream. She remembered when she had gone to the cinema to saw LEAP and promised her dad to become a ballerina and help the poor.

The weird thing about time travel is the limits. We can go forwards as far as we want but not backward. Traveling back from 'now' is impossible, as if the continuum was chopped right off.

Surprisingly, time could take man anywhere; time could bring the colony's wealthiest person to poverty. Time could take the healthiest person to death bed. She became confused about whether to become happy or not as TIME COULD CHANGE EVERYTHING.

Now the ladies were telling her about the terms and conditions and what she had to do...Zaini was becoming mentally prepared, sinking in her position, her brain commanding her how to present her best. Unusually, her interview took a lot of time and became so long.

When she came out, she was spurning herself. She thought she hasn't done good enough and now she would be disapproved.

It had been a few minutes since she had come out when a boy came out of the interview room and commanded her to follow him.

There were sitting both the ladies who she had met during the interview. This time, both the ladies were introducing themselves to Zaini very friendly.

"Can you extend your duration here in India?" she asked, and Zaini was surprised.

"Yes, but can I ask about the outcome of this interview?" she questioned, and the ladies smiled.

"We couldn't say anything about it yet, but we are extending your duration, and you need to stay here for a longer time," they told her, and Zaini was in a strange state of happiness. Her heart started pounding fast. “Have I finally been hired?” Zaini sat back and let the happiness soak right into her bones. She closed her eyes and savored the moment. For the first time in forever, her body and mind relaxed. Her dad's face came in front of her eyes. “I made it, Dad. I am the winner,' she said to herself.

After half an hour, she had been told the good news. The first call she made to let someone know about the good news was to Eliza.

"I knew it, Zaini. I knew you could make it," she was saying aloud on the phone, and Zaini was just giggling.

"It's just because of you, Eliza. I am standing here," Zaini was unable to calm.

"There is no need for such nonsense....Has the contract been signed?" she asked.

"No, it will be signed tomorrow," she told her happily.

"Oh, nice."

"When will your plane land?" questioned Zaini.

"At 1:00am," she answered.

"Have you told uncle and aunt about the good news?" asked Eliza.

"No, I haven't told them yet. I have just told dad about the extendedness. When I return to Pakistan, I will surprise them with a surprise," she smiled.

"Your life is going to change, Zaini...Don't forget to recognize me," she annoyed her, and Zaini laughed.

And she didn't believe in life-changing until she saw the contract in front of her eyes the next day on which there was written 10 lakhs only. Her hands shivered when she signed. It was one of the most significant contracts she had signed. It was not just a contract; it was the solution to all her problems. Life was really going to change. In this amount, she could transplant her dad's blood undoubtedly. She cried uncontrollably, and people there became anxious.

"Is everything alright?" people came and inquired her.

"Everything is fine. I have just become a bit emotional," Zaini laughed between tears.

Rubbing her eyes and cheeks like a child with both her palms, she wanted to fly to Pakistan and share this moment of joy with her dad.

And what if she weren't so intense? She wouldn't get this reward. Without any doubt, leaving the loved one takes much courage, but also that courage pays off.

The one who fears to stay in night

Can never see the silver moon.

The flower that refuses to bear sunlight

Can never blush or bloom.

*****

ACCIDENT OR MURDER

It was 2:30 of the night when she switched on the TV to see the news and how India's news channels look.

"PIA airplane F-707, which was going to land successfully at the India airport at 3:10 am, has been crashed as something went wrong in the system. It was a new airplane, and it was its first flight which became its first disastrous flight as mechanical defects have been detected," the news reporter was reporting one of the latest news. "We have found the airplane remains and the dead passengers in a jungle. It seems there was no time for parachutes, and in seconds, it was a fireball in the trees. All that remained is a mess of mangled metal," he was just saying all this without even taking time to breathe, "Fortunately, there were just 20 passengers, as it was the tiniest airplane, but unfortunately, nothing left other than ashes."

The news rolled over her slowly and painfully. There was not a single thing she could do about any of the crap news she just heard.

The sky has darkened; the clouds were no longer white or paler grey. Instead, they were blackened shadows that shift with the wind. There were times they moved just enough to reveal the full moon, but for the most part, this night will be without the benefit of silvery light.

Her room was also filled with darkness, and she started crying bitterly.

"My Sis, don't you have any manners? Your friend is standing outside the door, and you are not opening it!" Wherever she was looking, she was seeing nothing other than Eliza's face.

"Just today, just right now!" She was just sitting on the sofa crying incessantly for hours. Her grief was literally astounding. Her heart had been shattered harshly.

"Huff, you fright me so much that I jumped out of my…" Everything around her was in motion. At the slowest pace, the birds started waking up as the dawn was covering the dark night. She was unable to listen to the birds' chirping and was only able to stare at their movement.

"Just a plane crash could burn hollow souls into nothing but ashes on barren ground? And turn minds into a damp cold cave of morbid nothingness? OR it was a death that came, and the plane crash was just an apparent reason?" she questioned herself.

The clouds were floating as she saw outside in the open sky. Grey clouds parallel to soft cotton cheeks. They were filled with as much water as her watering eyes, or her eyes were more filled.

"Does life pass this much quick?"

"And life passes more quickly, we don't even apprehend that our time is progressing and we are coming closer to death. We don't even perceive and our last moment in this momentary world came...And...THE END."

In the hands of death,

When the angels are wrapped,

All that is left

Are the things that are said.

*****

Her phone was ringing, but as she was crying from the last night, crying silently, crying loudly, crying without tears, crying with tears, she was not receiving the call. The call was from the person she would never wish to talk to. Zayan.

"Hello," came a voice from the other side as soon as she received the call after the constant ringing of 10 minutes.

"Yes," she answered.

"Sorry to hear about the plane crash news. It was a really heart-rending one," he showed grief.

"Hm."

"She was so young. I am still not able to understand how this could be possible; it's unexpected," he continued.

"Hm."

"Now you are alone, and you alone have to handle everything. Every single thing depends on you now, and I am sure you can handle each thing so perfectly."

"Anything else," her patience was just going to terminate.

"No, nothing more."

"That's good. Bye," said Zaini and declined the call. The combo of the grief and the hate for Zayan made her incapable of bearing his rubbish anymore.

Grief, it feels like emptiness in heart, a shear of nothingness that somehow takes over and holds the soul and threatens to kill oneelf entirely. It gave her this heavy feeling like the world's weight was resting on her shoulders and there was nothing she could do to get out from under it. It's like this hole in her heart that was the shape of the one she lost, and that made her feel the need to wipe away any non-existent tears that she wanted to form but couldn't.

*****

"Well, well, well," said Zayan, "the work has been done flawlessly. Congratulations, Dear."

"Thank you so much, but how did you do that?" asked Alisha.

"Don't forget, Honey. In our society or in this sphere, everything can be done. All we need is money."

"Yes, but you just said of Eliza. What about the rest of the 19 innocent people who died?" she asked.

"Oh, Dear, that's not my fault. I haven't done anything; it was their bad fortune that dragged them to the mouth of death," said Zayan with facile.

"You are also right," she agreed. "But what will be the benefit now? I haven't understood that yet," she questioned.

"Listen carefully," he stated, "She is suffering from a great trauma now. She would take time for herself to heal. Then, her dad will die soon as he is not well nowadays. She wouldn't be healed from the first shock that another tragic circumstance will come that she would need to handle. She would get busy and will forget about us. Simple."

"Will you kill her dad also?" she asked.

"No, you don't worry, Honey. Now, I won't kill any of the innocent. It's just my prediction that he will die soon," he said with a laugh.

"I trust you," she said. "But is that this much easy," she asked curiously.

"Yes, it is, Honey, don't you believe me?"

"Of course, Dear, I do believe you."

"So, no need to worry, I am here. Everything will be fine. Zayan knows how to deal with each sort of situation," he said proudly.

"I am feeling proud of having you as a husband," she spoke.

"Haha, me too, Honey," and they both giggled.

*****

THE TSUNAMIS.

Abeeha slowly opened her eyes and pulled up her eyelashes laboriously. She could feel a lot of heaviness upon them.

She was surrounded by darkness, pitch-black darkness. She was lying as if her back was against the wall and her knees against her chest. It was as if she was stuck in a lot of stuff somewhere in a relatively narrow and dark place.

She blinked her eyes a few times; the situation remained the same, darkness and pitch-black darkness. She could just feel as she was in a cramped room where there were heavy objects everywhere.

Her right hand stretched as she tried to lift herself up. She pulled her hand, iron tinkled. She felt a handcuff on her right wrist; she was tied to the wall. She jerked her wrist vigorously, but nothing affected.

She was going through severe headache and backache alike. She has been bruised. She barely controlled herself and sat up straight with the support of the other hand. She twisted her neck, a tingle of pain arose instinctively. A moan came out of her lips.

When the eyes became accustomed to the darkness, she got to know that the walls were made of wooden slabs through which the moonlight was gleaming in the darkness of the night. She tried to recognize the place, but she couldn't.

A load on the left began to fall on her. She pushed that away with tiresomeness. Her hand became wet. She closed her damp hand towards her face to see. She was unable to see the color of the wetness but could smell it. It was blood.

She was frightened and started rubbing her hand with her clothes. She got to know then she did not have her coat that she had worn. The thought or the reality she was suffering from was so painful, leading her to faint. She had been kidnapped.

*****

It was 9:00 pm. She was trying to fall asleep, but it seemed impossible. Her head was filled with several thoughts, what if's continually flooding into her brain. She turned on her phone and scrolled through her Instagram feed, trying to tire herself, but it didn't work.

She decided to call Dad and reveal the contract's secret to share some happy moments to feel good. She was tired and wanted to let herself come back to life.

She ringed Dad's number, but it was powered off. She ringed again, powered off. She became anxious. She called her mother. She was not responding; she called again and again but still no answer.

At that instant, she decided to leave everything and went back to Pakistan. Something or a lot of things weren't okay. She was worried. It came as an electrical storm in her brain that, quite honestly, was painful.

The task for which she had been paid was finished that morning, and she was free to go home back or get signed for another work. She arranged the earliest convenient flight of 6:00 am and started packing her luggage. She ringed Zayan and told him about the flight so that he would come to the airport and take her back home. She became so busy, and she remained busy till her plane landed at Karachi Airport the next morning.

Zayan received her at the airport. She sat with him in the car. He started conversing, and she was just giving him short answers.

"You have taken a wrong turn; we can't reach home this way," Zaini interrupted when Zayan took a strange route. He remained silent.

He stopped the car in front of the hospital. Zaini thought he might have some work. She didn't say anything, but her sixth sense started alarming her.

"Mother is not receiving the call. Dad's phone is powered off. Why Zayan took me here? Is Dad alright?" Her blood ran cold.

*****

Zaini saw Dad lying on the stretcher, surrounded by the doctors taking him to the operation theatre. She ran towards doctors; her eyes were filled with fear.

"What happened to my dad? What happened to my dad?" she asked the doctor with a strange sort of fear.

"Pray so that nothing can happen," the doctor replied.

They hurried through the operation theatre, the wheels of the stretcher and her pounding footsteps the only thing she could hear. "Miss, you cannot follow them." The receptionist stopped her with a manicured hand. Her heart sank into her chest as the stretcher disappeared from view.

"All I can do is to choke out, as my mind is filling with a succession of horrible outcomes, each worse than the last," Zaini was saying.

"You must wait in the waiting room," she said in an educated but clipped tones. She watched through perfect mascara as Zaini sat dejectedly in one of the hard plastic chairs.

The hospital's corridor was deserted. The floor was like a dead person. White, lifeless, cold. She was sitting straight on the chair. The tears were continually flowing down her eyes.

All the time Dad was in the operation theatre, she was just sitting there. Her brain became paralyzed. It was like her head had been crushed by a big rock, as she was unable to think about anything other than her dad.

Tears were falling from her eyes in the form of strings.

"Pray so that nothing can happen," she repeated the saying of the doctor.

"What is praying? How to pray? And whom to pray? Is this the only way to cure Dad? But I have never prayed, and I don't even know how to pray. What should I do?" she examined herself.

At that instant, she remembered her father's sayings,

"THE HELPING DOOR IS NEVER CLOSED, AND THE HELPER IS ALWAYS, EVERY TIME WITH US. HE CAN DO EVERYTHING, HE IS THE BIGGEST."

"THE HELPER IS ALWAYS, EVERY TIME WITH US."

"THE HELPER IS ALWAYS, EVERY TIME WITH US," the lines were echoing in her head.

"My helper, please listen to me," she was crying with voice and without voice, "You know, Eliza was my best friend. She also died; now I have no one but only Dad. Please don't snatch him from me. If he dies, I will also die. Please listen to me, please save him, please return my dad back. I love him a lot," she was trembling with her face covered in her palms. "I am alone. I have no one to ask for help but you now. I have no door to knock except yours. My first hope is you, and my last hope is you. If you wouldn't help me, no one will. 'Coz when I was a kid, my father told me of you. He told me the Helper is always, every time with us. If you would take Dad, no one will give him to me. If you don't take, no one has the power to take him from me. Please, please return my dad to me, please." Each tear was like a ball of fire falling on her heart and burning it.

"Helper, I have no one but you to whom I would ask, and there is no one but you who could give. Please fulfill my wish, just one wish. I will never ask for anything else in my entire life then. Return me my dad's life, please. I will ask him about you and will do each thing that makes you happy. I will never make you angry, please cure my dadP please return him back to me." Hiding her face in the hands, she was crying bitterly. She never felt this much loneliness in her entire life. She never felt this weak, this much vulnerable, and this much helpless in her whole life.

How many hours passed, how much time spent? She didn't know; it was just getting dark.

She looked up and saw Zayan standing in front of her. She tried to control herself, but tears started falling from her eyes again. He placed one hand on Zaini's shoulder and said,

"He will be fine, he will. Don't cry, have you eaten anything?... You are not looking fine; I am bringing some food to eat." He went to the hospital's canteen, and when he came back, he was holding a biscuit and a juice.

"Eat something." He took out the biscuits from the wrapper and offered them to her.

"No," she refused. At the same moment, doctors came out from the operation theatre. Her brain stuttered, and she stood up writhingly.

"Let me see," he stopped her, went toward the doctor, and started talking with him. She was staring at both of them while standing restlessly. Every part of her went on pause.

"Okay, okay," ending the conversation while nodding the head, he returned to her.

"What was the doctor saying? Is Dad okay?"

"Zaini, the doctor has given me this. He was saying your dad was holding this piece of paper and was saying that 'this belongs to my daughter,' incessantly, means this belongs to you. It's yours," he said while giving her the piece of paper on which a number was written.

"What is this?" She held that piece of paper, saw the number, became a bit confused but then put it in her pocket, and then asked, "Leave it, tell me how is Dad?"

"He is fine, but you are not looking fine. Sit here and eat this." He let her sit on the chair again and offered her the biscuits.

"Oh, thank God, he is fine. My prayer has been answered," she leaned her head against the wall tiredly.

"Eat something..." At that time, even Zayan was not looking nasty to her. She ate some biscuits and drank some juice.

"Zayan, my prayer is not rejected. I asked the Helper much; how could this be possible that it wouldn't be answered?" she was saying and looking at the distant space in a lost way.

"Zaini, eat some more lest your health will deteriorate."

"No, you don't know how much I prayed, then how could it not be answered," her eyes were again filled with tears.

He just stayed silent, and she was speaking while crying with happy tears and seeing the empty walls.

"You know nothing can defeat a man unless he doesn't give up, and today, I didn't give up."

"But sometimes, fate defeats," he said very slowly. She was surprised. Zayan was looking at her and suddenly, her heart sank.

"What?"

"Zaini...Dad has died." The silence of the corridor broke.

*****

She stood up silently and started walking towards the exit door. She saw her mother sitting on the bench of the hospital's corridor.

"On the very next day you went, your dad's health had begun to deteriorate. He forbade to tell you. We took him to different hospitals, but his health was becoming worse and worse. Poison was found in his blood....and today...right now..." she didn't complete her sentence. Zaini knew what she would say next, but now, maybe she just didn't want to listen.

"They are not giving the body. They are saying to clear the bills first," told her mother.

Zaini was the money-earning man in her house, and she never regretted her role in her entire life. That moment, standing there for the first time in forever, she desired someone to be in place of her that would earn money, somebody else...like Dad...

Dad...the word dad made her aware of the world again.

"Yes, I am doing something," she said in a slow voice without even making eye contact with her mother.

When you are exhausted by the memes

And your inner voice screams.

When it's difficult for you to breathe,

And you need to ask Why me?

*****

"How much is the bill?" she went and asked the doctor.

"18 lakhs, 20 thousand," replied the doctor.

"18 lakhs. How did you make this much bill?" she wailed.

"Listen, Ma'am, this is a private hospital, the best hospital for cancer patients of the city. We were giving your patient the best aid at the perfect time. We operated him in an emergency. We gave him the best of the best medicines...You can see everything in the bills," he was elaborating mechanically.

"I will clear each bill, but not now. Let me take him; I will surely clear each bill," she was begging.

"Ma'am, I sympathize with you, but I don't own this hospital. I am also a worker here...I can't give you the dead body till you don't clear the bills," the doctor replied very smoothly but in a straight manner. Instead of her dad's name, she became cataleptic for a few minutes listening to the word dead body.

"We could give you some time. You may take loan from someone," he said while closing one of the files which was lying in front of him.

"And you will give time, not my dad!" started Zaini. He remained silent. Suddenly, she remembered the contract she signed, which was still in her bag.

"Here is the check of ten lakhs. You may take it right now; the rest of the bill will be paid in one or two days," she offered him that contract check.

"Your name is mentioned on this check. What will the hospital do of it? And we don't take payment in checks. We need cash payment," he refused and returned the check.

"But..."

"Why did you bring him to this hospital if you couldn't afford the bills? This is a minimal amount of a few lakhs. People pay bills of much more than this without any queries," the doctor said, letting her realize her status.

"We brought him here to save his life...It was acceptable at any cost...You didn't save it...We didn't bring him here so that he would die," she said and went back to her mother. It was the first time she became so harsh, and it was the first time her voice trembled while speaking. She was just going to burst into tears, but no, it was not the time to cry.

*****

"I said that we will clear the bills in one or two days, but the doctor disagreed on that. He was saying that he will give us some days so that we would take a loan from someone, but he will not give us the body till we don't clear the bills. Now what to do?" told Zaini.

"So why don't you give the money you earned in your job?" said mother sarcastically.

"I offered him the check of 10 lakhs also, but they are not accepting checks. They are asking for cash payment," she clarified.

"Oh."

"Don't you have a single penny for investing in your own husband?" said Zaini in the same sarcastic tone.

"Mind your language first, and secondly, I don't do any job so that I would have money."

"So what do you do all day and days outside?" she inquired. Mother had nothing to answer; Zaini's question made her speechless. "Why are you not answering me?" asked Zaini more loudly.

"Okay, I am telling, but not here. Walk to a place where no one can listen," she said and started walking to find a better place, and Zaini followed her.

"So, what do you need to listen?" asked mother after finding a perfect place to converse.

"The thing you are hiding," she answered straight.

"Well," sighed mother, "Zayan, the one who gave you the job is my husband. I had married him when your dad was diagnosed with cancer. And it was a love marriage, that's it. Now please keep your mouth shut, don't tell him that I have told you."

"Oh, nice love story," provoked Zaini, "but what will I get for keeping my mouth shut."

"What...What do you mean by this?"

"Clear all the bills today, or else I will tell this to Zayan," she played a game, or the situation made her a gamer.

"But how could I?" she was puzzled.

"That's not my headache," she said and went out of the hospital.

How circumstances change a person, she got to know about that on her dad's death. When her entire existence was just going to keel over, how strongly she put all the broken pieces back and handle the situation.

After the long day of being so alone, the pain didn't ebb. On the lonely night when she could not control herself, her eyes started glimmering with watery tears, and she felt as if the whole world was about to crumble. She dropped down on her knees and screamed with all her might. She sobbed, and tears flooded like the water rushes down from a waterfall. The only time she would stop was to fill her lungs with air.

She thought she would feel the knives in her back forever, the long blades slicing into such sensitive flesh. That was the day her brain felt electrocuted, so violently defocused, and the pain, the emotional pain, was so all encompassing that she simply existed as a matter of willpower.

Sometimes, the night seems so long that sunrise starts to feel like a myth. Sometimes, the clouds cover every last bit of light to the point where you wonder if the sun will ever be able to shine for you again.

*****

"18 lakhs, 20 thousand," said the doctor while counting the last thousand notes.

It looked like Zaini was a princess whose wound's ointment was the payment. Now she was able to get her dad's body back.

"Mother, I will go to India back and get on my work from tomorrow," said Zaini when she came back after having some vital conversation with the doctor.

"Oh, but isn't it too early?" she asked.

"Oh please, don't act as you care," chuckled Zaini, "Now I have nothing left here. At least, I can work there."

"Okay, as you wish," Mother agreed.

*****

PENETRATION IN THE WORLD OF BEAST

The girl became nervous as she found herself in an anonymous place. She calmed herself as her sixth sense let her know that she has been brought somewhere oppressively. She closed her eyes again and leaned her head against the wall. She wanted to think, a path, a way for escape, any source of help, and at that time, she heard a man saying;

"Boss will kill us; we just have kidnapped a few girls."

"We don't have enough time; let's go right now," said another man.

"First, we will try at the airport, then..." the voice was becoming slower and slower, and then she was unable to listen.

She tried to focus on their conversation. They were talking about the kidnapping. "Where am I right now? Am I still in Pakistan or somewhere else? And where are the other girls?" she thought.

She kept thinking for a long time with her aching head, but she could not extract any solution. It seemed like her head was spinning, and each door of help was closed.

A pale yellow beam of light came through the wooden slabs as the dawn had arrived and swallowed the darky night brilliantly. The load again began to fall on her. She tried to see what was it through that little light and was shocked. She was a beautiful girl with long blonde hair that fell on her. Her mouth and arm were bleeding, and something was reflecting from her sleeveless arm. Something was written on it. She contracted her eyes so that she could read the written words, and she read as SOLD.

She can feel the sweat drenching her skin, the throbbing of her veins, and the thumping of her heart against her chest. Her fingers were curled into a fist, nails digging into her palm. She couldn't hear her rapid breathing, but she could feel the oxygen flooding in and out of her lungs.

Hesitantly, she started looking in the surrounding, and her eyes gazed first at the ground, which was covered with blood, and then at the piles of girls lying around her. Some had edema on their face, some had scratches on their arms, and some were totally injured—unconscious, dead to the world.

Fear tortured her gut, churning her stomach in intense cramps. Fear engulfed her conscience, knocking all other thoughts aside. Fear overwhelmed her body, making it drastically exhausted.

First, there was a knock on the door, and then the door opened with a heavy creak. She immediately rolled her neck to one side and closed her eyes.

Someone came inside, bent on her, unfastened the handcuff with a key, and started dragging her outside by clenching her wrist, matching the attitude done with a wild animal.

He carried her into the basement, flattened her on the floor, and went outside.

A bearded, mustached man was sitting on a royal chair, on whose feet she was brought and thrown. The light was so dull, but it was enough for her to recognize who that man was.

"Oh, Dad, you are here..." she uttered.

"Hahaha, yes, Baby, I am here," he laughed. "Aww, my baby is bleeding," he said while seeing her hand. "But now don't worry, you are meant to be brought here for bleeding, My Dear," he said sarcastically.

"What..." she was perplexed.

He stood up from his royal chair, held her bloody hand fiercely, chained her to the wall, stared at her for a moment, and smiled. The dim light made his skin sparkle and glow. It stung and sent swells of pain through her body. A chin rested on her shoulder; he was breathing onto her ear.

"I'm glad I have you forever now. I'd call it destiny," he grinned.

She opened her mouth to ask why he was doing this, even though he was her father. But as his lips clamped down on her ears, he bit down harder and caused her to cry out. Two hands slid down her sides and landed on her waist, just above the hem of her jeans. She didn't know what to do. She knew this would be bad.

"I have already trained you for this."

"I don't want it. I haven't ever wanted it," she yelled.

"Okay, but, Darling, you can't erase the past...Not even when you don't remember it," he said ironically. His lips moved down to her neck and nipped at the tender skin. Her skin bruised so quickly, she knew it would make a mark.

"Does it hurt?" he asked carefully, looking at the colossal scar that trailed on her neck. It was reddish-purple in color and bumpy, raised above the skin so slightly.

"It did. Years ago when I first received it."

"I can't believe someone could do this to you!" he whispered and began to suck the skin furiously until she let out a noise of panic.

His stubby fingers curled in her hair. Abeeha was just going to lose her consciousness. As she closed her eyes, he bashed her head back onto the concrete wall demanding to open them. She was unable; she was shutting them over and over. He became angry and started beating her until blood ran from the back of her head and her head lolled like a doll.

*****

She was leaving home permanently. She was going to a place that had been her childhood cocoon. She loved her home and the community around it so much that for then, she could only bury the pain and hope to deal with it later. Those who would take her place were only walls, the streets only concrete, but there was love there for her. As she turned to depart, she felt a part of her soul imprint onto the walls.

"People leave home with their parents begging them to stay. Mine showed nothing but banal indifference," she thought. "For people, there are tears, parcels of food, and promises to send money to ease their transition. The only sound as I leave is the door banging behind me, caught by the wind. Somehow, I am forcefully glad as I have nothing left. It punctuates my exit, the biggest full stop of my life, nothing but a blank page ahead. I guess it's my fault I never tried to love anyone except my few loves who are no longer with me. I swear I will love my future children; they will never be just an ATM machine. They'll be treated as a being, and I will love them, give them what I never had."

It was 7:30 when Zaini left the house. She had a flight at 11:00 am. According to the airport's rule, she needed to arrive at the airport 3 hours before the departing time.

The plane took off at sharp 11:00 am and landed at the India airport in 2 hours and 12 minutes. She hired a taxi there as she knew where to go, put all her luggage inside, and started moving. The flag on the cab was fluttering violently in the wind. It was cute on the city streets, but on the highway, it was moving so quickly and noisily that she wondered if it could break away from the pole. She watched the cheap plastic bending and the flying flag as if it was trying to take flight. It stayed that way until the car slowed for the off-ramp.

She switched her attention to the changing scenery. It was a bit strange, as she remembered her hotel route flawlessly. The turn he took was unfamiliar to her. She remained silent and thought that maybe it would be any shortcut, but the path was becoming isolated slowly.

"Where are you taking me?" she asked with a stiff voice.

He adjusted the rearview mirror to see her in it and remained silent.

"I asked where are you taking me?" she asked harshly.

He stopped his taxi at a place where there was no chance of someone's arrival. There were trees everywhere, and it was looking as their existence was the only existence there.

As soon as he stopped his taxi, Zaini came out of the cab quickly regardless of taking her luggage and started running. He rapidly came out and started running after her, and in a few moments, he shot on her back.

The bullet entered as if she was nothing, just meat, bloody bones, blasting a cavity in her back as it burst crimson into the fading day. Her beautiful face was frozen, closing eyes, mouth slack, as she propelled backward. The light slowed, and the sounds became as if underwater. Aside from the beat of her heart, no muscle would move.

*****

"She was running, so I shot her," he told his boss.

He stood up from his royal chair, frozen. The room was filled with silence. His brain took a few seconds to understand what he was saying and when he came to understand... his eyes spread from uncertainty, becoming red with anger. He came nearer to him and BASH, slapped on his face hard. He wasn't ready for the attack and staggered to the other side, held the wall, put his own hand on the cheek, and saw him with obscurity—the one which was rapidly breathing and was looking at him with the same shock.

"You...you shoot her? Oh my God, YOU BASTARD..." he said while grabbing his collar and shaking him violently. "How could you shoot her? Where is she? Now we will not fetch a good price for her."

He left his collar and started roaming here and there. It was as if his mind had been blown away.

"Is she dead?" he asked him with the same anger.

"No, she is alive; the doctor who had cured the last one girl's head is curing her right now in room no.10," he told him the details.

He started moving towards room no.10. Along with the smell of medicines, there was a curse that was spreading everywhere. The night was dark...black and appalling. He entered the room and asked the doctor who had just sat on the chair:

"Is she alive?"

"Yes, she is," told the doctor.

"Okay...and what about Abeeha? Did she come to her senses?”

"No, not yet... Zaliq, you injured her so badly, but I hope she will be in her consciousness soon."

"That's good."

"But why don't you kill both of them? They will not give you much profit," asked the doctor.

"They will surely give me profit once they recover," he said boldly, "By the way, I never wondered, Zayan, that you could also work as a surgeon while running a dance academy."

"Hahaha. Well, Bro, I also never wondered that an honorable man like you could do such a despicable thing," answered Zayan, "Like kidnapping your own daughter."

"Shut up, she is not my daughter," shouted Zaliq.

"Whatever," said Zayan "Do you know who she is?" he asked while pointing at the girl who was shot.

"No," he shrugged. "She is my wife's stepdaughter," told Zayan.

"What...!" he was surprised.

"Yes, she is my wife's late husband's daughter from his first marriage. This girl is now an orphan," xxplained Zayan.

"So...Are you going to tell her stepmother, your wife, about her?" asked Zaliq.

"No, no...Love never existed for her in me, and of course, nor in her stepmother, and Alisha will even not think where Zaini went as she left home permanently on the day your assistant shot her."

"Oh, sounds cool," responded Zaliq.

"This summer saw the taking of not one but two daughters' lives," Zayan was saying in a way an anchor makes an announcement. "Though they both didn't die, of course, they are also not going to live their lives fully. They are just going to exist. Over the next few weeks, their wounds would heal, but their mind would shatter. They would be crying in dark places with wide eyes, shivering no matter if it would be warm or cold..."

"Oh, please cut the crap!" yelled Zaliq and went outside the room.

*****

MEETUP WITH BARBARIANS

A vague ceiling appeared as she wearily opened her eyes. She gently blinked her eyes so that the scenario became a bit clearer. Pain arose on Abeeha's face. It had returned with intensity as her sensations returned; she slightly moaned and turned her head.

She was lying on the bed in a spacious room. Another girl was lying fainted on the other bed, far from hers. She could not see her face. She tried to get up on her elbows, but her body felt as if it was jammed.

"Ouch," her eyes closed as the pain intensified.

"Relax, keep calm..." The doctor quickly came nearer to her.

She slowly blinked her eyes. This face, this face...she knew this face, but at that time, she was incapable of recognizing him.

"Where am I?" she closed her eyes and muttered.

"Do you need water? Or anything else? Is something causing pain?" he asked with care. She had heard this voice before, but where?

She blinked her eyes. The man in the dress pants, inclining over her, became apparent. Tall, sharp chin, brown hair...

"Where is my dad?" she tried to get up once again, but she failed.

"May I give you a glass of water?" This time, Abeeha looked at him carefully, "Can't he hear me?" she thought.

She tried again to get up, but what was the thing that was obstructing her from moving? Her eyes scrolled to her arms—both, from elbow to wrist, were tied to the clumps.

Suddenly, the aftermath of drugs and medicines seemed to wear off. She looked around in hysteria.

"Where am I?" Surprisingly and terrifyingly, she asked the man who was inclining over her.

"Do you want water?" he asked politely again.

"Where am I?" As soon as she said it, she tried to yank her arm hard, but the grip was so firm that it remained still. He straightened up, wrapped his arms around his chest, and looked at her.

"DO YOU WANT WATER OR NOT?" he asked. She dropped her head on the pillow and stared at him.

"Where am I? Where is my family?" she asked in a sluggish motile.

But he went towards the telephone, maybe to inform someone. In a few moments, the door opened, and footsteps were heard.

As she moved, the rested neck that was on the pillow, a blurred scene appeared. A bearded, mustached man was coming towards her. She was seeing a blurry image, but she could recognize the man: DAD. He came towards her.

"Don't," whispered Abeeha. Her eyes locked on the syringe in Dad's hand. "Don't," a bolt of panic shot through her, dizzying and sick.

Her limbs lurched uselessly against the cruelly tight clamps. It did nothing, as she could barely move an inch. Zaliq swept closer without care. The needle was a wicked-looking thing, and a cold, damp spread through the room.

"What is this?" she demanded.

Zaliq rolled up her sleeves to expose her arms, focused as he pressed the skin around the veins to test it.

"You could never forgive yourself for what you let me do. You think you can be free by getting the scholarship? Think again. I own your soul. You can't fight that," said Zaliq sneeringly and started singing,

Violation of your justice

Desecration of your love;

Penetration in your soul,

You are totally in my control.

"Dad, what is this?"

"It is a serum developed to seize control of your neural pathways. If you move, it can be excruciating. I suggest you take a few deep breaths and try to relax."

Her eyes were closing over and over, darkness, then lights, darkness…lights...

"I don't just want to kill you, Baby. I want to put you in a pit and add the shovels of dirt slowly until your Goddamn mouth is full of muck. I want to hear the suffocation of your cries. I want to know the second you don't exist anymore so I can savor it. I don't care if you're sorry for the mistake you didn't make. I don't want to hear it. When I was a loving person, you came and took what was beautiful in me and made it into what I am today. I hope you're proud; it's all your handiwork," Zaliq spoke with coldness. He grinned, showing yellowed teeth amongst the stubble. His eyes were wide and unblinking, his thin lips turning upwards into a smile and one hand injecting the serum in Abeeha's arm.

The man came nearer to Zaliq, "At least open her hands; she is sick and injured. How could she run in this condition?"

"You don't need to tell me, Zayan, what I have to do and what I don't. Though you are my brother, mind your own business," he said and stared at him sharply.

"Okay, but..." the words mishmash and her mind sank into darkness.

*****

She let her eyes rest a moment to allow her senses to rise so that she could accept the reality. She had heard the whole conversation, but she kept her eyes closed and acted as she was still unaware of the world.

She came to know by the conversation of both men that the doctor was Zayan and the man named Zaliq was his brother who was torturing her own daughter. What kind of extreme brutality he would do with the girl and with her also, she could imagine, and that would be so much devastating.

She tried to see the girl from the corner of her eye when Zaliq went outside and Zayan was busy tidying his sitting place. All she could conclude was an unbelievable truth that the girl was Abeeha and recognizing her was not a fact of surprise since she was her teacher and teachers never forget their students.

Zaini thought of the day when Abeeha had called her, and suddenly, her voice was muffled. She kept calling her, but Abeeha was not answering. She had declined the call and thought that maybe the signals had dropped or there was an emergency due to which she couldn't respond. She had left a message of good regards and started packing.

"Why didn't I think of something serious when she was not answering?" she regretted. "Why didn't I think of that 'Has my message reached Abeeha?' As she didn't answer the good regards I sent her. How could I be so irresponsible for my lovely kid? She was going to travel first time alone. Oh my God, for how long she is here and how much she would have been tortured till now, and I was just unaware of all these things," she grieved.

The room was filled with light, but there was still a strange terror surrounding the room.

"I need to go to the washroom," said Zaini aloud with boldness. Zayan came nearer to her as soon as he heard.

"Hope you have discerned me," said Zayan maliciously.

"Hold on to your hope, absolutely, you are right," answered Zaini, "But right now, I am not in a mood for any kind of debate."

"How could you be!" said Zayan sneeringly, "I am opening the clamps. If you do not come out of the washroom in 5 minutes, compulsively, I would have to call out the guards, and then you can imagine what they will do with you."

As he opened the clamps, she sat up and lowered her feet to the ground.

"Ouch," her face was lined with pain.

"Take my hand," Zayan tried to hold her for support.

"No!" she jerked.

"Hey, Darl, I am not asking you to marry me. I am just trying to save you from the injuries that could be caused by falling."

"Oh, please, cut the crap," she said and moved on.

She reached the washroom with quivering footsteps. Taking the wall's support, she came to the sink. Holding it with both hands, lips clenching in pain, she looked up in the mirror.

"What could I have done wrong that I am here today?" she opened the tap, filled both hands with water, and poured it on her face.

"I will definitely get out of here, and then I will kill all of you one by one with the utmost torment. You all will be a sign of admonition for the world and tell what happens to such wicked people," looking in the mirror with red eyes, she muttered.

"Right now, I've been injured by just a bullet, but I can imagine that what could you do to me and others. And I am sure I wouldn't be here alone. There will also be other girls, injured more than me, less than me, killed or sold," the water drops dripped from her face while she was thinking.

"I am ready for all the holy crap you will force me to go through, but I will never forget anything. Each of you must be held accountable once I get out of here, just once," she looked back at her wound.

"Where am I? In my native land or somewhere else?" her mind began to wander.

She rotated her neck. The washroom had no window, but upon the shower, there was a small loophole. The view was blacked out by painting the glass black, and the glass was locked. The loophole was so small that she couldn't even pass out her arm. How could someone pass out from it? She looked around...soap, shampoo, tissue paper, towel...there was nothing in that washroom other than this.

"EVEN WHEN THERE IS NOTHING TO HAPPEN, SOMETHING DOES HAPPEN,"

she remembered the quotation she had seen on the banner.

She came to the towel stand, took off the towel, and started pulling the steel rod. A little force and the rod came in hands.

Then she went to the shower, lifted the neck, and checked the height. The roof was not so high, she held the shower hose from one hand, lifted herself up, and put her foot on the lower tap.

"Ouch!" The pain in the wound increased. Clenching teeth with pain, she forced herself to stop screaming and climbed up.

She put another foot on the hot water tap and extended her steel rod-held hand. The rod began to touch the glass; she couldn't unlock it. With all her might, she struck the head of the rod on the glass. One, two, three...

The door began to knock vociferously—the angry voice of Zayan and then the guards' roaring. Without even thinking and listening, she was repeatedly striking the glass with the steel rod. The back wound began to bleed, and the pain increased. She kept hitting, but sufficient force did not exert due to pain. The stroke did not seem more substantial, and the glass remained ineffective.

Blood started streaming, and at the same time, the sound of glass breaking came. Unbelievably, a hole formed in the middle She threw the rod, extended her hand, and started taking out the pieces of glass. An interstice was made.

The door's lock broke. The guards came inside. As they came in, they spoke out invectives. Zaini glanced once at the blazing sun. Maybe she was at the top of the building, that's why she could see the whole city from there, but her heart began to sink —terror and surprise fell in her eyes.

Below, a guard hit that same iron rod on her thigh. A muffled scream came out of her mouth; she was going to fall, but the other guard pulled her down at the same moment. Blood was oozing from her back; the glass pieces had wounded her hand and caused it to bleed.

The beast-like guards dragged her to a big hall and tied her on a chair even though she was still bleeding.

"Leave me, let me go," she moaned.

One of them tore a piece of duct tape with his fierce teeth and stuck it on her mouth.

"Ummm...." She started moving her head here and there, to and fro, her voice oppressed. They went outside the hall without paying any attention.

She looked all around the hall. It was enormous, a big sofa on one side and a fireplace on the other next to which she was tied to a chair. The fire was burning in the fireplace. The dark orange-red fire was burning the pieces of iron rods on which some English words were written. She saw it keenly and added all the words she was able to read, but maybe she didn't want to read or she was afraid of reading.

For saying, they were just four words, but deep down, those four words weren't just. Those four words could destroy her life. Those four words could kill her and make her dead for her entire life while living. Those four words could treat her no better than cattle or pigs. Those four words could just feed rations only enough to keep her from starving. Those four words could get her whipped if she didn't work hard enough. Those four words could beat her until her back would become a bloody mass of open flesh in front of everyone else. Those four words could just let her sleep on bare wooden floors with thin blanket and could let her rise at the crack of dawn to work all day. Obviously, by the grace of those four words, in a world of cruel slavery, she would have been targeted for rape several times while the world and her remaining so-called family would be unaware of her or they wouldn't be interested in saving her. Or they wouldn't have enough time for saving her or maybe deep down her so-called family would also be enjoying her. And those four words were just SOLD.

Beside the fireplace, there was a small brazier. A thick liquid-like honey was boiling in a pot over burning coals in it. The smell was spread everywhere, of that viscous brown liquid. Maybe it was wax.

She dropped her neck, her courage was running out. She has been there alone for so long, and there was no way out, but:

"EVEN WHEN THERE IS NOTHING TO HAPPEN, SOMETHING DOES HAPPEN," Zaini remembered.

She was pressuring her mind. No matter what, she didn't want to give up till her last breath. And deep down, the truth was that not giving up was her most significant victory.

"THE HELPER IS ALWAYS, EVERY TIME WITH US," she suddenly remembered.

"Please, Helper, help me please," she was saying with tear-filled eyes. Her wish was not fulfilled the last time, but maybe this time, this wish would be fulfilled. Perhaps, the helper would help her now.

Being near to the flame, she could feel the heat. She was seeing the fire whose red embers were soaring in the dark surrounding. The warmth was increasing; she felt like her entire existence was burning in flames, and that time, her brain revived her dream.

"Did that dream come true today? Or that dream was some kind of warning? But warning for what?" her head began to spin.

Long hair were scattered on her waist and shoulders. She was not even able to tie them up. Drops of sweat were glistening on her neck and forehead.

Suddenly, the door opened. She turned her head and looked. He was the same man who injected the toxin into Abeeha: Zaliq. Holding a bag in his hands, which he threw on the table, he entered inside and came nearer to her. With one hand, he turned the chair to himself on which Zaini was tied, and with the other, he grabbed the edge of the duct tape and pulled it.

"Aha...Do you think you can run away from here?" he said caustically.

"Please, let me go!"

"I let you go!" he laughed sarcastically and went towards the burning brazier.

"What wrong have I done?" looking at his back, she demanded in a pleading tone. He was standing in front of the fire; the oppressive wave of heat became inferior, she got some peace.

"You don't understand! Of course, I don't want to do this! But your initiative of freedom forced me to do this. And you know it as well as I do that it has to be done and somebody's got to do it," he said trenchantly.

"Please, let me go!"

"Poor girl, poor people," he shook his head in denial, picked up a rod, and looked at it upside down.

"No, I could pay you ransom money," she cried.

"I don't want your money. I want your pain," he turned to her as he spoke.

Without answering, she was continually seeing the terrifying, burning iron rods. Her heart was pumping as fast as it could, head spinning, lungs bursting, and the body screaming for a way out.

"Please, let me go!" she screamed.

He brought the burning rod close to her on which SO had turned into embers. He shut her mouth with one hand, and that one frantic hand was enough. She felt her ribs heaving; her chest was straining to inflate her lungs. Her head was a carousel of fears spinning out of control, each one pushing her mind into blackness. She wanted to run.

"Can you see this burning rod? I am going to just burn your arm with this, and then you will see how nicely we will treat you. But man, oh man, am I gonna feel bad about it!" he said maliciously.

Zaini started impelling her neck left to right, right to left. Zaliq was going to burn her with the burning rod.

"Let's do it!" he evinced and took the burning rod nearer to her arm. She felt the burning embers' heat just below the shoulder. She began to shake her head in distress.

At that second, she asked the helper for help with extreme anguish. Whatever happens, she just wanted to get rid of that savage beast, Zaliq.

Her mouth wanted to open, to scream. Her unblinking eyes popped like a fashioned toy doll. A bead of cool sweat dripped down her back, and her skin became pale.

The savage beast, Zaliq, pressed the burning iron rod on her arm. A heartrending scream came out of her throat. She was in the throes, but he was still mangling the sizzling rod. The flesh was burning. It was the worst kind of fervor injury that was descending into her soul.

When you meet a new character,

And that's no less than hell,

But you still need to live with it;

And that's how life spends.

She was screeching, she was crying. After a few seconds, he lifted up the burning rod. She was totally burned. He went towards the brazier and threw that rod in it. Zaini looked up at him with swollen red eyes and came in a wreck. He was holding in his hands another burning rod whose English written words LD had become embers.

"No, please...For the sake of someone you love...Please, no...."she began to push herself back in agony, but the ropes had tied her so tightly that she couldn't move.

"No..." she was screaming with terror. He came nearer to her, giggling. Besides the highlighted burned letters, he mangled another burning rod onto the same arm.

"All the blood looks good on you. It really brings out your eyes. I think I should add you to my collection," he vocalized while pressing harder.

The pain began to reach the limits of her endorsement. She was screaming shrilly with pain; she felt that she was about to die with anguish. It was a burning wound that penetrated deep into her body.

After a few moments, when he pulled up the rod, her neck lolled on one side. She was hardly breathing; she was about to lose consciousness. Her face was full of tears, but she had no power left to cry more.

She had no idea what the raging beast, Zaliq, would do now, but she knew that she would not be treated nicely. She looked at him painfully with closing eyes; she had no power left to scream some more. Her whole life was animating in front of her eyes, like an animated movie. Childhood days, memories, father—telling her the beautiful stories. The scenario changed; she was sitting in the car with her school bag, going to school for the first time with her hero, Dad! She was crying as she didn't want to leave her superman for the school's sake. Now she showed her new dresses to Eliza with great pleasure, and she was smiling at her excitement. Now she was playing with her students; Mishal, Abeeha, Abrash Sofia, and Yafiah on the calming green grass...soft...soothing...green grass...

Zaliq clutched her hair from the back of her neck and pulled her face up.

"Now, have you come to know the outgrowth of our disobedience?" he asked violently.

She looked at him with stonkered eyes and spat on his face. He stunned, parted her hairs from his hands, and moved back, picked up the burning pot by the handle from the brazier—the pool of heated molten wax.

"You...You miserable shrew!" yelling at her with his opprobrious tongue, he came towards her and raised the pot on her head. Her eyes widened in fear.

"No...No..."that was all that came out of her lips, and the ferocious beast, Zaliq, poured the heated wax pot on her head.

The hot, boiled wax furiously fell on her hairs and began to roll down from all sides. A torturous shriek came out of her lips, as the boiling wax corroded her scalp. She was screaming in a wild manner, trying to free her tied hands. Zaliq became flummoxed, and in that state, he pushed the chair mightily and Zaini overturned on the floor near the fireplace.

The room filled with fumes, and the wax started cooling on her head. Her head became extremely heavy, her eyes were closing, and the blood was coming out of her mouth. The fumes were increasing. She was so close to the fireplace that the fire flames were about to reach her.

With cheeks laying on the floor and closing eyes, she saw the scenario, the ferocious beast, Zaliq, was holding a gun in his hands. She thought that he was going to shoot her and kept laying there. She heard the turbulence of gunfire that went into the back of her mind to a place of ignorance. He had shot himself.

She was left in the room, but also the fire, the fumes, the blood was with her. The flames had reached her, and the last thing that she saw was her shirt that had started burning. She saw her white shirt turning into orange-red embers; the fumes were everywhere. 'Maybe the reality of my dream is the ending of my life,' she thought. She understood that she was going to die.

*****

A STEP BEYOND

There was a little mistiness when she opened her eyes; she blinked her eyes two or three times. The scenario became more apparent; her hands were not tied this time. She slowly got up on her elbows and started looking at every nook and cranny.

"I was not in this room last time when I had opened my eyes," she thought. She didn't remember how long she had been sleeping and how many injections she had been injected. Abeeha didn't even know where she was. She knew nothing.

The roof was white and the door also. There was a washroom, a window, a water dispenser, a wall mirror, two small tables, and the two ordinary single beds. Abeeha was laying on one, and on the other, at the end of the room, there was another girl. She wanted to see her, but she was unable to see clearly. She raised her neck and finally saw the face.

The scene was quite staggering, shocking, really. Abeeha's mind was sent reeling, unable to comprehend or process the image being sent by her eyes. She looked away, then looked back to see if she was still there. She was Zaini, Ma'am Zaini.

Her hands were frail, subdued and greyish. Her hair was wispy over the scalp, and the bandages were fastened almost everywhere.

"Ma'am, Ma'am, can you hear me? It's Abeeha," she raised her voice and called her. She didn't answer. "Maybe Ma'am is sleeping or unconscious," she thought.

Zayan was not there at that time. Instead, he was opening the door and entering; she looked up at him. There were guards outside the door, and further may be the dining hall. All she could see was just that, and the door closed.

He filled the disposable glass with water; there were medicines in his hand. He came to Abeeha and gave them to her. She refused to take them.

"Take them. You need to take care of yourself because you can never get out of here now."

"Why? Where am I? In which city am I? Why don't you people tell me?"

"You should ask instead in which country am I!"

And on his words, her whole being came on the mode of pause.

"You are in India... Is it shocking? or do you want to hear another shocking news?" asked Zayan.

She was just staring at him—unintentionally.

"Zaliq, your dad, shot himself!"

Five simple words constructed of simple letters spoke courteously through his English accent cut through Abeeha. A reel of a film played in her head. Her eyes burned, but she didn't mourn the way daughters do.

"Okay! You may go now," she said in a low voice.

"Don't you have any grief for your father?" asked Zayan woefully and sat beside her.

"Grief of what? Man is mortal," she answered straight.

"Are you still angry with your late dad?" he asked slowly.

"Please, don't act as you care; get out of here," she replied

But all it takes is one trigger, and everything comes crashing down. The world seems darker and painful again.

"Fierce? Still? For just what he has done to you in these few days?" he asked again.

"Can you please stop?" she begged.

"Didn't it hurt?" he questioned again.

"Not 'hurt,' hurt is just a four-letter word, short, almost cute-sounding," she answered in a fragile tone.

"Awww, did that hurt?" he spoke in a sarcastic vein.

"No, it didn't hurt me. It destroyed, obliterated, annihilated, desecrated, shattered, and demoralized me, but no...It didn't hurt me. It didn't hurt me at all," she become brittled, "Now, please go."

"Okay, okay, I am going, but remember, you can't escape from here. Can you see her condition?" Zayan said while pointing at Zaini, "She had tried to escape, so it's better to stay here quietly. We will provide you all the necessities, and you will know soon why you have been brought here," he said and went outside.

*****

She opened her eyes slowly; the white roof was in front of her eyes. Her head was on a soft pillow, and the blanket was wrapped up till her neck. She took a quick look at the room. It was not the last one; she saw Abeeha, maybe she was sleeping. It seemed to be the early morning ‘coz the sunlight was beaming through the white blinds, presenting the morning sun against the cruel faces.

She again shut her eyes and put her arm on them. In the past few hours, she had been in a trance; she had screamed a lot, cried a lot.

She remembered she had been brought here, the injections and the drips, the bandages, and the half-conscious state. She remembered everything slowly but didn't forget that she was still in that doomy place.

The door opened with a slight squeak; maybe it was not locked. The footsteps' noise came nearer to the bed. Zaini didn't move nor remove her arm; she knew who it would be.

"Good morning!" said Zayan and put both the breakfast trays on both the side tables; she didn't even change her position.

"I knew you are awake, eat this," he let Zaini know.

"First, you eat in front of me," Zaini demanded while removing her arm from the eyes.

"I have done breakfast," he replied.

"Then take it out from here. How do I know whether you have put the poison or not."

"Everyone gets the same breakfast," he told her.

"I don't trust you, and why should I?!"

"Then kept lying on your bed. I will return back for lunch," he grumbled and went back.

She took off the blanket, got up, and put her feet down. As she stood on her feet, a wave of pain arose in her back. She had several injuries on the back, knees, arms, and shoulders.

With naked foot, she walked to the wall mirror. Her reflection looked very tired with dark circles under swollen eyes, profound purple edema below her right eye, several scratches on the chin and forehead, and swelling on the right side of the lips. She moved her fingers from top to the last nip of her hair. They were not the same as before. They were thin and short, and the glow was gone. The wax was washed, but the pain she tolerated wouldn't be washed away. The moment when Zaliq shot himself was the same moment when guards had come inside, and one of them had extinguished the flames. But as much as that savage beast, Zaliq, had burned her, that burning will hurt her entire life.

She was wearing the same clothes; she rolled up the sleeve of the right hand from the left up to her shoulder. The black ashen-like four words inscribed on the upper part of her arm were still, 'SOLD.' She repeated, to whom I have been sold? She questioned herself, “Do I need to suffer the white slavery now? And wouldn't the brutal and inhuman acts be brought to the fore? Do I quietly need to accept everything? Does the torture that was and will be inflicted on me would remain a secret?”

*****

As Abeeha changed the crotch, her eyes opened. Zaini was standing in front of the mirror, lost in her thoughts. The light was beaming through the window; she called out her teacher, Zaini.

"Ma'am," she turned back in shock and smiled slightly after seeing her.

"How is your health now?" asked Zaini and sat beside her.

"Better..." she paused, voice stifled. "How do you know I was not well?"

"How can you be fine while living in this cruel place?" questioned Zaini.

"How did you get here?" asked Abeeha.

"The way you would have got here, not willingly, outrageously," she answered. "Did they do anything wrong to you?" Zaini asked with care.

"THEY didn't do anything to me. Just my own DAD tortured me a lot, and now, fortunately, he is no more," replied Abeeha with brittleness, "What did he do to you? You are looking badly injured."

"I am just injured. Don't worry about me," said Zaini firmly.

"Will we never be able to get out of this wicked place?" Abeeha was severely broken.

"We will get out of here, soon," she made a hope, "That's what I've been thinking since morning."

"So, is there a way out?" she asked hopefully.

"Yes, there is, but for that, we need to be strong. Are you ready?" asked Zaini courageously.

"Yes, I am ready!" she said with determination.

"Okay, so listen...First of all, we need to be strong. We can't fight with just our words. Our hands, our feet, our whole body should also fight. We need to be physically strong. Secondly, we are not in our homes, and I am sure this is not our country..."

"This is India," she interrupted.

"How do you know?" she asked curiously.

"The doctor told me," told Abeeha.

"Who, the doctor? Zayan?" she asked again.

"Yes, maybe."

"Well, that's good. At least, we got to know the country in which currently we are. This will help us a lot," she said brightly, "Okay, so now, secondly, this is not our native country, and here we should mentally prepare ourselves first for each kind of cruelty, brutality, inhumanity, slavery, and barbarism. We need to be mentally healthy. Thirdly, even if we face extreme viciousness, even when there is no way to get out of the darkness, we need to be emotionally intense, even if we both get apart. We will not cry as babies do. We will get up and fight again. We do not belong to this white painted walled room. We are not meant for any kind of slavery; we belong to a higher place that we can't imagine," Zaini was encouraging her with zeal for getting out of that violent place. Abeeha was listening carefully to her, "So, are you ready to accept all these terms. Should I tell you the plan?" she asked again.

"Yes, Ma'am, your student is ready," she said with the firmness of purpose.

"Okay, that's good, my kid. So, we will..." She was telling her the escape plan, and Abeeha was listening to her keenly.

"Will we escape just right now?" she asked after listening to her.

"No, not right now. We both are not healthy enough for this risky escape. We need to be salubrious first."

"So, when?" she inquired again.

"In one or two days," she replied.

"Oh, that's fine."

"Now, I am having an extreme headache, Kid. I am going on my bed to take some rest; you may also," she said and kissed on her forehead. "Don't worry now, we are together, and together we will get out of here. If anything bothers you and I am sleeping, you may wake me up," she said with the provision of protection and care, stood up, and started taking steps back to her bed.

"Ma'am!" she called out, deep in thoughts.

"Yes!"

"What are we?"

"We are just made of tiny cells on Earth. Till now, we are living with no understanding of our existence, and our lives yet have no deep meaning."

"No, I meant...Forget it, I am sleeping," said Abeeha, as she laid on the bed quickly and acted as fallen asleep.

*****

LIVING THE FIRST TIME

The day passed. Zaini and Abeeha both spent their day as the prisoners do. Zayan had come in the afternoon and offered them lunch, but they refused as they didn't know about the ingredients that made up the food. They were just drinking water as Zayan himself had consumed the same water that was offered to both of them.

The sun had gone to rest, and the lingering light was obliterated by the rapidly falling night. The moon had taken its place as the darkness surrounded. The once white sky had transformed into a vast expanse of jet-black that had engulfed everything.

Abeeha was awake; the thoughts were accelerating inside her head. She wanted them to slow so she could breathe easily, but they won't. Her breaths came in gasps, and she felt like she will pass out. Her heart was hammering inside her chest.

The room spun, and she squatted on the floor, trying to make everything slow to something her brain and body could cope with. She felt so sick. She wanted to call an ambulance, but she was unable. She couldn't understand what to do, everything was spinning, and it felt as if the ground was melting under her feet...Blackness...Creeping blackness...She was on the floor in a ball in the fetal position, her breathing shallow and quick.

She crawled to Zaini's bed,

"Ma'am," she gasped and extended her hand upward so that she would move and wake up.

She didn't wake up; maybe she was intoxicated after being drugged.

"Ma'am," she gasped again. She was unable to control her breathing rate.

"Whoa!" she woke up nervously. She could hear Abeeha saying something, but she sounded distant and muffled. "What happened to my kid?" she asked, came down, and sat beside her.

"What happened?" she asked lovingly. Abeeha's heart was still hammering inside her chest.

She was shaking uncontrollably. She felt Zaini's hands gently rest on her shoulders and that was when she thought she could burst out and there was someone who would listen to her. That was when she felt that her childhood desire is going to be fulfilled. She always wanted to be those little babies who cry and scream when they could not explain their feelings; that was when she felt she was not alone anymore.

"Abeeha! My dear, what happened?" she again asked her affectionately, but she didn't answer.

Zaini wrapped her in a warm swaddle of her chest and arms. There was something so warm, something that felt right. Abeeha let her body sag, her muscles became slack. In that embrace, she felt her worries losing their keen sting. She felt optimism raising its head from the dirt. Perhaps, the hope had been there all along. But without some love, it was trapped, like crystals in a stone. Abeeha felt her teacher brushing her back with her piano playing fingers; she kissed her gently. She didn't want to leave; it felt as if in her arms, all her pain went away— mental and physical, mostly the depressing pain.

"Ma'am," she paused, took a deep breath, and said, "Could I stay in your arms forever, safe from the world's evil people," and she started crying.

The tears fell down and fall off her nose.

She went to a place which nobody knows.

Crying felt good, mostly when they were tears that didn't want to be pushed away. They weren't drops of sadness, no. They were more like the feeling of relief and freedom streaming out from the hurt eyes. They were temporary cleaners to wash away the pain. She never cried, but that night, under the protection of that beautiful person, she felt she could let the floodgates open. She stared at her and continued to let her pain run away for the moment.

After the heart-soothing, quiet, warm, long hug full of love and tears, Abeeha was feeling something she never felt, something she couldn't explain in just a few words.

"Now tell me what happened!" asked Zaini

"I originated from a cruel place," she sighed..."I was raised in barbaric conditions and faced brutality," said Abeeha after a long silence and then again started shivering.

"Who is the cruel one?" asked Zaini while grabbing her shivering hands with her soft ones.

"Dad!" she stifled.

"What did he do to you?" questioned Zaini.

"My dad was a bit of a drinker. It's how I got my bruises," this is how she started telling. "I don't think that he is truly my dad. If he was, then he would give me everything—his heart, his soul. Instead, he wrapped me in iron and beat me with a stick that I had willingly surrendered with a loving heart. In doing so,

I crippled myself, came closer to a human snake with narrowed eyes and a forked tongue. In the beginning, he only beat me, but then one night, he came to me. That time, I was seven maybe. And that was the day when my worth, my privacy, my personality, my confidence had been taken away. It lasted for approx. twelve years. I am nineteen now," she took a deep breath, "At the beginning of this year, I was seriously tired of that turd. I was encouraging myself for months to stop it somehow. And one day, when there was no one at home except him and me, I had a dust-up. Suddenly, my mother came and I told her everything. He had been threatening me a lot from the day I was beaten the very first time. That's why I had never told anyone before. After that action, he attempted to kill me many times, but fortunately, I always survived," her voice was shivering. But instead of stopping, she continued, "I was so much happy of my scholarship, as I had thought that I would get rid of him. Yet, no, I was wrong. His last attempt was kidnapping me and torturing me till death, but I don't know how the tables turned and he committed suicide." And suddenly, she felt her ribs heaving as if bound by ropes, straining to inflate her lungs. She tightened her hands that had been grabbed by her teacher.

Think before you say

Daughters need their fathers,

Think of the girls who pay

Ransoms of being daughters.

Think before you think

She is Dad's little princess.

Think before you think

He is the hero of that Lil.

"Honey," said Zaini and waited for the response while seeing into her eyes, which were seeing something Zaini couldn't, something they suffered.

"My kid, my girl, he is gone now, and now no one could do such a callous thing to you again."

"But..." she crumbled, "He was my dad!"

"He WAS your dad, Dear," she made her understood tenderly while holding her hands.

Abeeha didn't answer. She was speaking with great pain and was no longer being spoken to. Words had left her. Zaini stared into those empty eyes that wanted to say something, but maybe the words were inadequate for saying anything. Everything was slow, as if she was stuck underwater.

Zaini was waiting for her to speak, but as she didn't, she called her out again, “Abeeha!" but she remained numb.

"Say something, my honey..." said Zaini, but her mind was blank and her eyes wide. She stared at her.

"Do you know what's the worst thing?" she asked her teacher after the silence of 10 minutes.

"What?"

"The insecurity. The internal brokenness that only a person exposed to my suffering can experience. Those mental scars are a tapering factor in domestic life's serenity. They cause agony that can only be seen on the inside. The pain that no one else sees. Every facet of my personality is denigrated and shunned. I am less than nothing, not even as loved as an object to be used... Every look that came my way is laced with contempt, along with the scars of my trauma. I could never let anyone near to me. I want to forget, but I can never escape from such an awful, horrific, distressing experience. This experience has caused

PTSD. My social life doesn't exist; my room walls are my best friends. Every night I calm myself...I mean calm myself after the nightmares...Every morning, I wake, not knowing why, I sit for a minute and rewind it all in my head, playing it over and over again. I ask myself so many times if all my life till now could be a dream. After all, he was my dad," her voice trailed away as her words were unwilling to take flight...

What a daughter can do

If her father is the anger in her words,

The ghost in her smile.

What a daughter can do

If her father is the pain in her tears,

The fear in her bones.

What a daughter can do

If her father is the hurt in her heart,

The reason she keeps a dart.

What a daughter can do

If a father who is meant to stay hers', raise her,

Breaks her.

Zaini kept holding her hands, waiting for her to speak more, encouraging her to talk as sometimes speaking up to someone could lessen the soul's burden.

"In my nights, he is a monster, and in my days, he is the same. There are times I can't tell the nightmare of my reality from the fiction of my nightmares. He beat me with the earthly 'gifts' he had. With a lot of ease, he crushed every ounce of my self-worth I gleaned. He didn't choose me for love or cherish, but to whip and destroy," there was sadness in her eyes, "Now, there are nights I lay in my bed pushing my face into the long toy snake. All it takes is one trigger, and everything pulverizes inside me. I felt myself in those horrific days, and then with an act of great courage, when I open my eyes, I find myself right where I was with just a toy to comfort me...I wish my words have the power that you would understand how painful it is to suffer and to suffer after all the sufferings, but all I know is that they all are just WORDS," said Abeeha with tear-filled eyes and trembling voice.

"My sweetheart, I can understand. I am going to protect you; no one can hurt you now. I am and will always be with you," said Zaini delicately. Abeeha said nothing; they both were staring at each other.

Zaini wrapped her arms around her shoulders and pulled her close, gently rubbing her arm. Despite the heaviness in Abeeha's stomach, she fluttered at the feeling of hugging. She sunk into the warmth of her side. In her embrace, the world stopped still on its axis. There was no time, no wind, no rain. Abeeha's mind was at peace; her touch made the room warmer somehow, her future with her seemed a little less bleak. This was the love she'd waited for, prayed for. She inwardly thanked God and hugged all the tighter. A love like this was to be cherished for life. Maybe, she was the home.

*****

ON TO BETTER THINGS

Before dawn, the eastern sky was filling with blended tones of rosy pink and sandy yellow. It was a subtle way to welcome a new day, a new beginning. They both were standing in front of the window and gossiping about the things they never did. Suddenly, the mighty sun breached the horizon, and the sky exploded with beautiful colors. At that moment, the firmament was more vibrant than any fresh mango or tangerine could ever be. Sunlight filled the air, gently kissing the faces of all good things that are wild and free. The peace felt in those fleeting seconds became eternal as they both drew the deepest breath and lost themselves in the morning view.

Zaini and Abeeha both hadn't slept the whole night. Zaini had told Abeeha about the way she was burned, and now they were tired. Therefore Zaini made Abeeha sleep first, then she also went for sleeping. They were taking rest because they didn't know when will they get the opportunity to take a break after this morning and where will their next morning be or will they be able to see the next morning's sun or not. They wanted to take it in its entirety, as this was the day when they both had to escape.

They both woke up by the knocking of Zayan at the time of lunch.

Slowly and reluctantly, Zaini uncovered her face. She blinked, closed her eyes, and blinked again. Streaks of sunlight penetrated the window and blinded her. She sat up, dragged her feet off the bed, rubbed her knuckles onto her eyes, stretched her arms above her head, yawned, and opened the door.

Dressed in a black dress-pant, Zayan, nearby him were two guards standing alert, came inside, put the food on the side tables.

"Why didn't you open the door in the morning?" he asked.

"We were sleeping," told Zaini.

"Sleeping is a good habit, but excessive sleep is not," stated Zayan.

"Thank you," responded Zaini, "But you know it already; we will not eat this till you do not eat in front of us."

"I will not, and lemme see also that for how long you two don't eat," asserted Zayan and went back with the guards.

"Now, he will return in the night. Before that, we need to run away from here," explained Zaini.

Abeeha's muscles felt weak, just like her energy. She let out an exasperated sigh and then a loud yawn, ready to continue the day.

They both together lifted one bed and placed it on the other. Zaini stood up on the bed built by the two beds. The walls were quite low that her hands reached the tube light. She was loosening the nuts of it by the fork that came with their lunch, twisted it several times, and the nuts along the tube light came in hands.

"Are you sure there will be any path?"

"The place in which we are is kinda like a prison, and these kinda prisons always have some escape routes. And many times, they are found in the walls. I have studied this all," she described.

She gave the tube light to Abeeha so that she would put it down. She could see something strange where the tube light had been placed, a kind of iron sheet or something like that. She started moving her hand on that peculiar thing and... "Got it". There was a tiny button that couldn't be seen but could only be felt. She pressed it, and straightaway, the sheet slid showing a black space.

"We now need to climb into it," described Zaini.

"But I am scared."

Don't ask her why she didn't rush.

As sometimes, a bird spurns to abandon.

Even when the cage displays evacuation

Or you try to take it out of prison.

Then you may earn the actual reason.

"Abeeha, we need to do this for running out from here," she stated, "And we will, as we don't belong to this prison."

"Okay, I am ready," after some moments, she said boldly.

Abeeha climbed up first and then Zaini did. She tried to see what it was through the light of the room that was glistening inside a little. It was an elevator shaft. Without any lift, but the shaft was built fully. They were at the top floor and they had just a way of crawling down.

After climbing into the elevator shaft, Zaini closed the iron sheet. Pitch-darkness fell; both began to grope carefully and started moving down.

A little later, their eyes became accustomed to the darkness, and they were able to see the pathway, iron bars, and rods. The middle portion of the elevator was empty. They needed to move slowly and carefully, or else, no one could even find their dead bodies there.

"I can't," said Abeeha after continually crawling for fifteen minutes.

"Abeeha!" While grabbing the iron ladder-like rails, she took a deep breath, looked down at her, and said, "Life will not give us this opportunity again; that's why be quick."

And the fact that everyone knows that even in a state of extreme trouble and distress, one can survive if one doesn't give up and doesn't lose hope.

Hope is when they realize they can still move to get the position they deserve. That there is a possibility they can escape the darkness that has been engulfing them. And with that, the sun will come out from behind the clouds.

With the depth of the breathing in the endless nights,

Keep hoping you are approaching the morning lights.

*****

The prison-like building stood tall and painted white with the mart at the basement—lighted to its fullest.

They both reached the dark elevator shaft's ground after descending continuously for 25 minutes. Now, they were standing at the front of the closed-doors. The doors weren't well-built and seemed fragile, but they were still unable to break them. Each way of getting out seemed closed. It was less challenging to grope the iron rods and move down than climb up again. They could just get out of it by breaking the door; how? They didn't know. They didn't have any kind of weapon, not even the knife they got with lunch as they forgot it in their prison-like room.

The dark elevator shaft seemed desolated. Multiple feet below the earth's crust, they were trapped. And many floors above them was Zayan, seated relaxed, was drinking his hot tea with its absolute delight, unaware of both of them...

"I need to get out of here, please!" said Abeeha who was sweating as the result of the suffocation. She was gasping for breath. Tears started streaming down her face. "Please, please!" the voice was sinking, the heart was sinking.

"Abeeha! What happened? Don't give up. Remember we do not belong to this wicked place; we will get out of this, so soon," said Zaini encouragingly.

Abeeha leaned against the wall and sat on the floor.

"Help me, please. I am just going to lose my breaths," her voice was mostly subsided, and tears were flowing down her face.

Zaini tried to look around with a thumping heart, but it was so dark that she could not see anything. She started scrabbling at the walls like a blind person. She felt that the walls were covered with rods. She held a rod and began making efforts to take it out. She was pulling it with her full potential, but it was jammed. It did not even move a little. She left it, saw Abeeha, who was struggling to breathe, and again started scrabbling at the walls. She felt something, a thing like a rod but exactly not the same, less tightly jammed than the last rod. She started pulling it, exerting all her energy. And finally, that rod-like thing was in her hands; she was going to hit the door by it...

"PLINK

PLINK

PLINK..."

A strange sound made Zaini turn her head. She looked everywhere, back forth, left-right...around, who was making this noise? “Maybe I am unable to see because of the darkness,” she thought and again started scrabbling in search of the thing that was making noise.

Her hands got wet when it reached the place from where she had pulled out the rod-like thing. Water was dripping from a small hole. It seemed as the thing that she pulled out was attached somehow with a water line, and now the water was filling in the elevator shaft like the water fills the bathtub. There was no way from where the water could stream out. Shortly, the water will reach the top of their head, and they would die.

"What is happening?" asked Abeeha as she quickly stood up. This time, there was fear and horror in her voice.

"I don't know, Abeeha, what to do. I also don't know," she also gets fretful.

*****

The water reached their mouths. Zaini's hands turned red as she was continually trying to break the door with that rod-like thing. They were going to lose themselves.

The water rushed to their head like it owned them. It was cold and murky, stealing away the air that could save their fragile turning body. Their entire body was throbbing; their lungs felt as they've been set on fire. They held their breath as long as they could, too long in fact, red and black splotches danced in front of them. Even in that state, Zaini was continually trying to break the door.

Abeeha felt her brain fuzz with the onset of asphyxia. She tried to open her mouth to breathe, but only got water. Slowly, black began to seep in at the edge of her vision. Then, ever so slowly, everything faded away. Painfully, quietly—she didn't want to die like this, but it was too hard to try to fight. At that instant when death was overpowering them, Zaini hit the rod-like thing in the center of both the doors with all the strength that was left in her. One last time, one last try, and the water began to flow throughout the door. Slightly.

When you have been fed up,

And you want to give up.

But staying strong is the only thing.

You could do that time must.

The water came at their shoulder levels, and Zaini again started hitting the door. She didn't want to give up till her last breath. There was a slight tremor in her forceful hands; she was breathing with difficulty. She glimpsed at Abeeha who was forcefully opening her eyes. Zaini didn't want to also lose her. She didn't want to lose the child she had always been hiding in her wings. She did not want to lose the last reason for her survival.

One...Two...Three...With a strange noise, the door opened a little more to the right. Suddenly, the water overflowed, but still, she was unable to see the outside scenario. The door had opened a little. Zaini grabbed the edges of the gates with both hands and tried to open them, teeth grinding, the veins raised of her arms. It started to hurt, maybe her hand was injured, and it was bleeding.

The water was continuously flowing. Slowly the door slid more. And now, there was enough space to get out of it. She left the door and looked at Abeeha. She was lying with face down on the wet floor. She felt that her heart would stop, her feet chained for a moment. Zaini leaned towards her, straightened her; she was cold with closed eyes and purple lips.

"Abeeha..." she patted her face.

"Abeeha..." she called her name and put her hand on her neck; she was breathing. She was alive. Slowly she opened her eyes. Tiredly, Zaini looked above, closed her eyes, and took a deep breath, unaware of the outside people who were looking at them with curious eyes.

*****

When the flow of water decreased, people ran towards them. They both got confused, but then after seeing such a crowd and the groceries outside, Zaini guessed it would be a shopping mart. People would not know of anything that had been happening various floors above.

"We...We fell in this elevator shaft...and...and the water line burst," said Zaini with a trembling voice.

Many of the faces just listened and went. Many offered a hand of help, and few of them say something to themselves. Maybe they were wearing Bluetooth headphones and speaking to someone.

*****

Zayan was sitting comfortably, scrolling Instagram, smirking after seeing his increasing followers when his phone rang. He raised it towards the ear.

"What are you saying? How did they reach there? They were trapped on the top floor by the guards and some gadgets," he spoke on his phone with shock.

"According to them, they fell into this elevator shaft, and the water line burst," said the man from the other side.

"Just keep an eye on them," he roared and declined the call.

For an instance, he remained still, but then he gathered everyone and told them what to do.

"No, no, we would go. Just tell us the way outside please," said Zaini when she saw the few odd-eyed strange people and an accommodating lady asking them to come to her home for rest.

"Abeeha, build your courage. We have been caught; hold my hand and please don't leave. We gonna run. Put on some speed," whispered Zaini in Abeeha's ear and held her hand, telling her about the plan ahead. She stood up, getting ready to rush, as this was now the only way.

As they took a deep breath, Zaini took the first step for running. Then Abeeha took the second, and they started running. They knew that some people were chasing them, but they couldn't stop to look at them. They ran like eagles soaring across indigo skies and a herd of cheetahs racing through verdant meadows. They didn't know where they were nor where they were heading. They had no idea what time it was, and they had no clue what day it was. All they knew was they had to keep running forward. Not stopping for anything.

They were pursuing, and they both couldn't stop them. Some had guns in their hands, and some had knives meant to twist in their guts when they would get close. Chasers had been running in a scattered way. Run and hide, rinse repeat. Zaini and Abeeha's heartbeats were just about to explode, their minds scattered mess.

You are meant to proceed with life.

Even your life is torturing you.

But deep down, you don't know.

You are saving yourself from blues.

"Don't get scared," she said to Abeeha while running. She was full of fear herself, maybe deep down, she was encouraging herself. "They would be taking twisted delight in our fear. We should not get caught, or else Zayan now would plan to hold us up as an example, to strike fear into others, but we won't be his to butcher."

"I can't run anymore," said Abeeha. Her speed became less; they were still chasing, chasing from different directions.

"No, we would run until there's no skin left on our feet," said Zaini and pulled her so that she would run fast.

"And then?"

"Then, we would crawl," replied Zaini.

And suddenly, it started raining. The pitter-patter of the rain created a shield around them as the only sure way to escape was to bolt in a storm. The rain fell softly as if it knew of the hardships both behind and ahead. Each droplet alighted their skin with just enough coolness to command their minds to the present, pull them away from the pain of the past and the uncertainty of what was to come. The beads over their face joined in, washing over them in a delicate cascade of trickles. Zaini raised her eyes to the grey layer that touched every mountaintop. There were more to come before the skies cleared—of that, she could be sure.

They ran through a maze of buildings and winding side streets as the sky rumbled, and heavy rain bounced off the cobblestones. A storm smothered the sun, greying the world around them. Now, they could see the chasing people farther from them. Their dainty slippers were caked in mud, and the shower had battered their braided hair into a tangled mess.

Suddenly, Zaini's feet slipped, and she fell. The people were far but still chasing them. They got a chance to come nearer to them. She stood up, and again, they started running. Her breath came in small spurts, hot and nervous. Her slender fingers curled into a wet fist, swinging forward as if it would make her faster. Behind them, they could hear the baying howls of the dogs and jeering laughter of their enemies.

"Please, Helper, let me live," Zaini cried aloud, and it started raining more heavily. Maybe so that the antagonist couldn't see them clear and would lose them from their vision. Zaini and

Abeeha both were throwing themselves forward. Their lungs and heart were pumping, panic trembling in their exhausted limbs.

The pitiless rain was falling without a break, making roads a shallow river. A vile pain spread throughout Zaini's chest like a deadly infection, and her lungs beseeched her to stop walking. Abeeha was likely in the same condition. They stopped for a few seconds to take breaths. Their knees felt like rubber as they were running for hours. Helpless, they walked on, their feet dragging noisily on the wet surface, each step triggering a rush of pain in their chest. In a while, they were going to start running again. Abeeha looked back,

"They aren't chasing us anymore," she gladly told her.

"What!" Zaini also looked back. Despite her feeble condition, her lips curled into a smile with the realization that they had escaped.

They felt smug at the victory. Zaini and Abeeha had really made it. They were free from the filthy clutches of the cruel people. They were finally going to find their home, a home whose wings had not yet been torn by the evil people. A home still thriving, still breathing without restrictions, or so Zaini hoped.

"People like us who have resisted or attempted escape are always tortured and some even killed," she was telling Abeeha happily, sitting under the coolness of the tree. "Assailers are ruthless and merciless. We have been lucky that we escaped." They were gossiping now freely; they were now free, independent.

Not all of the kings make the evil burn.

Not all of the cards can be dealt with fun.

We can shuffle, and once the shuffling has begun,

Can't this shuffled deck make the table turn?

*****

ANOTHER ABORTIVE JUGGLERY

"Abeeha! How are you now?" asked Zaini after an hour of amusing talk when the night fell, and the rain stopped.

"I am shocked," answered Abeeha.

"Why?"

A few moments of silence passed; their eyes were fixed on the ground.

"I have never really thought that I could ever get out of my destructive home. When we are a child, our childhood should be rooted in love, compassion, and understanding. Mine was rooted in insecurities."

"Mine also," she closed her eyes in agony.

"Why? What happened to you?" Abeeha looked at her and asked her.

"My child, we all somewhere and somehow go through some hardships. We all suffer and what we become through that suffering is our identity. The suffering differs from one person to another."

"Ma'am," she sighed, "The guilt is still growing in me. He told me that no one would ever love me. And other than this, his other ruthless words are still engraved in my soul like a tattoo that is so difficult to eradicate. I felt I was the reason why everything had happened to me."

"My dear, you weren't the reason at all."

"Nothing in life can ever get better," Abeeha became fragile. "I see how my face looks without any makeup on. I see how my chin looks when I look down at my own reflection. I see how I look when I wear my old clothes. I see how my thighs jiggle when I walk or run. I see how my body looks when I look at my scars. I see how my arms sag when I have them up; I see how my acne looks when I wash my face. I am not just BEAUTIFUL ENOUGH."

"Honey," said Zaini lovingly to Abeeha, who was staring at the ground, "You are beautiful. You deserve love, you are stronger than you think. There is a lot you can do, and YOU had to go through that trauma because you had the potential. Don't ever underestimate yourself."

"But..." she stopped for a while and then continued, "Days come and go, and I am still living with grief, can't stop floating memories in my head. I am lost in a book of riddles that has no brief. I am sick and tired of my life, just believing I am a burden, thinking I am cursed, doing suicide attempts, feeling so numb. I am sick and tired of the depression, the anxiety, the panic attacks. My head is no less than shit, and I seriously wanna get rid of it," her eyes filled with tears.

"My dear, so get rid of it. Get out of this dark tunnel. Cross this darkened tunnel; the light is waiting for you!"

"But how? I spent years and years with the fears that I am still living with. How could I get rid of it so easily?"

"You could. You have the potential; this life is a journey where we have to fight our fears and move on," she encouraged her. "My love, I can't heal you, but I can help you heal yourself.

In the stillness, you can let the tornado that is your pain slow down. You can begin to take steps forward, to learn that life is okay. The skitter-scatter mind of yours is looking for solutions, a way to live in peace and thrive. Your mind is powerful, and it will devote itself to finding a way forward that works for you. I know it hurts, Kiddo, I know. Try to move, walk, paint, write, enjoy sunshine, nature, and birds, cut out negative media, and know I am always loving you so very much."

"I also just love you," asserted Abeeha.

"So, turn your pain into something beautiful. I know you can do it."

*****

Sitting comfortably in the crossed leg position, he saw the guard standing in front of him worryingly. They had chased them as long as they could but returned when they realized they both have run away.

"What will happen now? They both escaped."

"I have given their photos to the police. They have started their search. They are Pakistani terrorists now, and this whole building will be now a shopping mart. I have sold it, so there will be no evidence left that we have kept them in this prison and tortured them."

"Evidence!" he looked at him uncertainly. "How does the evidence matter? They will tell everything at their homes, and then your notoriety would be must."

"Hahaha, there is no one left in their home; to whom will they tell?"

"Seriously! That's mean. You have closed all the doors that would lead to your destruction."

"Yes, this time also. No one can harm us," he said proudly, "This time also, Zayan has handled everything."

*****

They both had closed their eyes and provided their heads with the support of a tree. As sleep is such a thing that it could come at the scaffolds, gradually, their bodies had become loose, their minds had sunk, and they didn't know at what time of night they both had fallen asleep.

Finally, the sun rose, filling the sky with shades of orange and pink. Peach and magenta, amber and rose, radiating hope, a new beginning. Another chance to live. The start of a brand new day.

Maybe, the scorching light was the reason that Abeeha woke up. She flustered, looked at herself, and then looked around. Zaini was already awake. The golden plate of the horizon in front of her was beaming such a bright light that Abeeha's eyes closed on their own. She immediately dropped her face in her hands.

The morning was bright, and the traffic was much more than it is usually in Pakistan—jammed roads, yelling people, and noises.

"At least, I am seeing this situation of roads for the first time. Pakistan is much better than this," said Abeeha to Zaini when her eyes got accustomed to the bright lights.

"Yes," she nodded her head in affirmation. "We were independent in Pakistan. Here, we are not. This is our opponent country and we don't know what a ploy Zayan would have made to catch us. Now, we have to get out of here; we aren't completely liberated. We are still in an invisible prison," she emphasized. "Do you remember what we will do now?" asked Zaini, "Don't forget about our plan ahead."

"Yes, surely, I do remember."

"Then, we are moving towards another risk," she stood up, and Abeeha followed her.

They both wore a cap to hide their faces, which they had got last night from the dustbin. They both held each other's hand and started walking, walking at a higher pace.

They were immensely sweating, but they didn't stop. The light was spread everywhere, and it was too hot, just as the sun was at the quarterstaff. They kept walking fast on the roads, streets, in search of a better place.

They neither found a better place where they could stay for rest nor found the telephone booth so that she could call the number that dad had sent her in his last moments. Indeed, this number could help them. From early morning, they were just walking, and momentarily took rest. It was afternoon and they were tired of the searching.

Cautiously, they stopped at a place. It was a garbage dump. They cleaned a small area and sat there; they didn't feel crummy. They had prepared themselves for worse conditions than this.

They both sat there for several hours, the body stiffened. They both held a sharp piece of glass that they found from the garbage as a dart. There was sweat on their faces; even a light gust of wind straightened them out.

Suddenly a strong wind blew, and the garbage flew over them. Abeeha and Zaini quickly started removing the wrappers, shoppers, and the other trash. Suddenly, a poster wafted over Abeeha and touched her hands. She unintentionally turned it over and became shocked upon seeing it. It was a poster of two Pakistani terrorist girls, a phone number was also written, and additionally, the prize of finding was 50000 Indian rupee per girl.

*****

She became mute, and at the strange muteness of Abeeha, Zaini, who was cleaning herself, looked at her,

"What happened?" she asked, and Abeeha was just gawking at the poster.

Zaini took the poster from her hands to see what it was that she couldn't stop staring. As soon as she saw it, she also became frozen, but she understood in a minute that they didn't have enough time to waste.

"We need to find a solution as soon as possible," said Zaini to Abeeha and made her aware of the world.

"Yes," she answered with cold sweat.

After a few moments, some people approached the heaps of garbage beside them and began to pick up the trash. They were probably the garbage collectors. Just before their arrival, Zaini had torn the poster into pieces and signaled Abeeha to react like they are sleeping. Maybe, she had seen them from a distance.

They looked over them, but neither had they given any kind of attention to them nor they acknowledged them, as they thought of the millions of beggars who sleep in the same condition. They felt that they would be two of the millions and left after the completion of their work.

"Abeeha, there is only one way left now!" said Zaini.

"What?"

"Are you ready to listen? Because that is the only way left or else these Indians would find us soon. And because of the word 'Pakistani terrorist', they could even eat us raw," Zaini told.

"I am ready," said Abeeha firmly.

"We need to change our identity. We will cut our hair."

"But...but how can we do that," she panicked.

"Abeeha, we have to, and we will."

"But...But, what will be the benefit of it?"

"In the poster, our pictures are representing that we belong to a rich family. And now, you may see our duds, our condition does not seem to be less than a person without two pennies to rub. Half of the identity depends on our long hair, and we would lose it by cutting them. Moreover, we would look worse than craptastic; no one could match us with those pictures," she gave her a brief description.

"Okay, nice plan, but..."

"Don't forget, my kid. We pledged of being strong, to remain stable from whatever situation we go through, and of not giving up."

"Okay, that's fine. I am ready for that also," she said with a fragile voice.

"Don't worry, Kid. Soon, we will be at a better, at a higher place," she tried to light up the extinguishing lamp.

"When and how will we do this?" asked Abeeha.

"When the sun will set, and the darkness will fell, and with the succor of this sharp piece of glass."

"Okay, I am ready, ‘coz I am robust," she said bravely.

"That's my kid," applauded Zaini.

*****

The night sky stood an inky canopy of darkness freckled only by the fewest of stars. Just hours ago, it had been a blue summer's day.

"Are u ready?" Zaini looked into Abeeha's eyes and asked.

"Yes," she took a deep breath and replied.

"Okay, then let's start," she said and pulled her hand towards the hair. Abeeha followed her with quivering hands.

The occasional hoot of a hidden owl was the only sound to permeate the silence until a chorus of cutting hair with a sharp piece of glass echoed into the emptiness of the night.

In 15 minutes, they both were done with their cutting. They looked at each other. They were not looking less than freaks; a girly structure with a boyish face, nothing could be more hideous than the faces so disfigured.

*****

WHEN THE SUN COMES OUT

Night melted away. The morning wasn't grey, but by soothing lavender and brilliant amber, the colors merged into neon pink and peach. The majestic sunrise, then red-orange glow seeped over the horizon as if the light itself was being poured from a molten sun—powerful rays were flooding over the landscape. Whether morning or night, India's traffic always remains the same, but birds' chorus broke the city traffic's drone.

They had been waiting for the morning for so long that they barely believed their eyes that it was really the beginning of the new day. It was the day when they could freely find their way. Free from the fear of being caught, as they were not looking like the way they looked before.

They had found a bag, pieces of sharp glass, a map of the city they were in, and two large black fabric pieces, all from the garbage dump. Abeeha kept the pieces of glass in the bag and hung its handles on her shoulders. Zaini had the map in her hands. They were wearing clothes, but additionally, they both had covered themselves and their head with pieces of black fabric.

They stood up and started walking, finding their way. The map reading was quite tricky, yet it was also the easiest way. Their appearances were deceiving. They looked like ramshackle beggars, their clothes were extraordinarily nasty, and their slippers were ripped with bare soles upon the walkway. Their appearances were not reflecting the vulnerable selves.

Walking barefoot for so long, over the rough city with rocky pathways, had toughened their feet. The skin that was once so tender had more resistance to the path's roughness, but the worst part was walking through the alley. That's where all the druggies were; one needle poke, and you could be infected with all manners of nasty things. Your feet could be cut and bruised by the end of it. Then they could ship you off to who knows where. But, fortunately, in the alleys, as they walked with the fastest steps, they weren't poked by them at all.

Barefoot was not a punishment, but the constant alert walk was—alert as they were not in their native country but their opponent one. Whatever they could do, they did. As looking different from the poster pictures, now they just could be cautious.

"For how long we need to walk more?" asked Abeeha tiredly.

"Don't know, Abeeha, but there will definitely be a way of getting out from all these somnolence days," answered Zaini.

"I am so tired. My legs are sore," mentioned Abeeha with pain.

"Mine too, but regardless of the soreness, it is time to appreciate the fragrance of the air, the sweet summer perfume we missed in the cold prison days. I never have ever walked without slippers or shoes, but now I can travel without them. I don't mind at all."

Soon after Zaini ended her phrase, they saw a pet Labrador running wolfishly, and a boy aging maybe fourteen or fifteen was running back to her. It seemed as the rope was mislaid by him. An idea clicked in Zaini's head.

"Abeeha, just don't run. This dog can be the means of getting us to our destination," said Zaini in a low voice.

"This dog!" Abeeha was amazed.

Zaini didn't reply. Instead, she picked up a stick that was on the zebra crossing, looked at the Labrador, showed it to her, and threw it far in the trees. Instead of running forward more, she ran back and about ten seconds later when the boy breathlessly reached near both of them, she leaped from the trees with a stick in her mouth. Zaini sat down and spread her hands in a way it looked a bowl. The Labrador put the stick in her hands, and two of them, the boy and Abeeha, were just seeing the show.

The Labrador's head was smaller than her neck. She leaped like a puppy and then pushed her body into Zaini's as soon as she was close enough. In seconds, her hands were covered in slobber, her tongue of sandpaper almost dripping with every lick. Her big brown eyes and her golden tail were swishing like she just got all her birthday wishes at once.

"How did you control her in just seconds?" the boy asked surprisingly.

"I know what she wants. I also had a Labrador when I was of your age," answered Zaini and threw that stick again, farther from before.

"She wants this slimy stick thrown down the path, not once, but over and over," told Zaini.

"I am so grateful," he thanked. "How can I help you?"

"Can you help us? You are a lil boy," spoke Zaini.

"Tell me, I will do my best to help you," said the boy in a supportive manner.

"I just wanted to call a number. Do you have a mobile? Can

you?" queried Zaini, and the Labrador returned.

"She's just too damn cute," said Zaini to the little boy and curled the fingers around the stick to feel the cool dampness. She released it at once and then saw the boy who had already taken out the mobile phone.

"Here it is; tell me the number. I will dial it for you." And at that moment, the world seemed like a paradise to her.

"+009198..." she started telling, and Abeeha neither said a word nor even moved.

"Who are you to him?" asked the boy when she ended, "I mean, who are you to Uncle Umar?"

"Me..!" she became confused, and the Labrador returned again. She sat down and cuddled her, thinking of the answer. She didn't expect such kind of question; she didn't know who Uncle Umar was.

"He is our relative," said Abeeha when she saw Zaini puzzled.

"Oh, that's great; I can take you to his house," said the boy.

"Can you? Do you know him?" said Zaini. They were amazed.

"Who doesn't know him? He is an Indian philanthropist and humanitarian who founded the foundation that runs the world's largest volunteer ambulance network and various homeless shelters, animal shelters, rehabilitation centers, and orphanages across India. He is called inside and outside of India as an ambassador to 'true Islam," told the boy.

"Oh," Zaini tried to hide her open-mouthed situation.

"I grew up in his house. I am an orphan; let's go there," said the boy.

"Yes, sure," said Zaini. They both—Zaini and Abeeha—saw each other.

The Labrador returned. Instead of throwing the stick, Zaini gave it to the boy, and she went to him, her master. He tied the rope around her neck, and all of them started moving.

They both felt as blossoms spread over them. Then they felt their lips stretch wider into a gaping grin and eyebrows arch for the sky.

They wanted to thank eternally for the one who showed them the light, for the graceful persistence when they had lost their way. Gratitude felt like such a tiny word.

In the storm, there is always a lighthouse, the direction in which to swim. There are days we feel like we have drowned, yet we can swim. We just need more strength to move. When we show our courage, we bear the things and suffer the situations that seem to be the most tragic. That is when we see something or someone shining in the belief that we could be more substantial, there is a way out, and we could keep moving on. That person or that thing cannot fashion a boat, nor take us out from the waves, but it can show us the direction and can tell us 'how to win life's challenges.'

*****

It was the kind of movement that spoke of a mind married perfectly to itself, and the world around it seemed confident, focused, and reverent.

They were walking through the forest, and upon the forest floor so woven with ancient tree roots came a light filtered by the bouquet of foliage above it, which were softened, verdant, and freshly aromatic. Abeeha tilted her head upward; the pines were several houses tall, reaching toward the golden rays of summer. Birdsong was coming in lulls and bursts; the silence and the singing was working together as well as any improvised melody. A new smile painted itself upon her face, rose-pink lips semi-illuminated by the dappled light. Her legs were on walk, body and mind— both on autopilot.

"How far is home?" asked Zaini from the boy, and Abeeha came back to reality.

"After this forest, we will cross a fair, and then by crossing some streets more, we will be at Uncle Umar's home. It would take approx. 30-35 minutes."

"Oh!" It was morning, and she couldn't expect the unknown home until brunch.

The forest was formed by the towering gentle giant trees made from simple seeds with mud, water, and the sun. Soon, after crossing the forest and few streets more, the crowded segment of the fair started. They were walking by, making their way through the crowd, and in 15 minutes, that fair also came to an end. They turned onto a street—the only street that was filled with silence, their existence was the only existence there, and their walking noise was the only noise there. After crossing that street and some more, the boy stopped in front of a large modern house and said,

"Here it is!"

The house looked as it was newly renovated. The windows were huge; anyone could see into the house from a distance as they both were eyeing. They could see the white, glossy surfaces and the newly painted walls.

"Don't you want to go inside?" asked the boy when he found both of them staring.

"Yes, yes, sure," replied Zaini.

He knocked on the door, which was opened by a guard.

"Who are they?" asked the guard while the other guard took the boy's Labrador to where other Labradors were playing. Neither the boy said anything nor the Labrador barked, as they both knew this had always been the case.

"They are uncle Umar's relative," replied the boy.

"That's charming; let them sit in the guest room. I am calling uncle."

"Sure," replied the boy, and they all sat there.

The house was a series of rectangles constructed of steel and glass. It was unapologetically modern. The roof was flat, and there was no visible chimney. The walls were fashionable shades of white, and the floor was polished white and glossy. They could see the entire house from the place they were sitting in. There was no clutter of shoes or jackets, no mess of any kind. The only organic matter insight was white orchids on the dark cherry coffee table. The kitchen was large enough for the chefs' army; there were two ovens and acres of brown flecked, white granite to prepare food. Each room was en-suite with a king-sized bed and a walk-in wardrobe.

******

"Can I say a thing, if you don't mind?" asked the guard respectfully at the door of the guest room.

"Yes, sure," said the boy.

"Actually, uncle is offering Salah, and I can't disturb him. So, you all may sit in the same room where he is and meet him when he finishes his Salah," told the guard.

"Yes, sure, no problem," said the boy.

They both were very nervous though they didn't express, as they were at an unknown house, waiting for a strange man to meet just because they no longer had a place to live. They could not even live like beggars as the country had declared them the Pakistani terrorists. Once caught as a terrorist, they neither could live their lives fully nor die peacefully. That unknown man was just left for them as Zaini's dad conveyed her his number; he couldn't have sent it for no reason. He could help them in some way.

Sitting on the prayer mat, he was offering Salah when the door opened slowly, and they all sat behind him on the sofa set.

"Uncle, some relatives came to meet you," announced the boy.

Uncle placed his trembling hands in the place of prostration to perform prostration.

سُبْحَانَ رَبِّيَ الأَعْلَى.

Translation: Glory is to my Lord, the Highest.

He recited the words with a shaking voice; the tears were falling and falling incessantly, a blurry image everywhere.

"They are two girls," he announced once again.

The voice was coming right behind him; he raised his tear-stained face and recited:

اللَّهُ أَكْبَرُ.

Translation: God is the greatest.

Tears blurred the whole scenario. Words were coming out of his lips in the form of sobs.

"Uncle, I know you normally cry when you stand in front of our Rabb, Allah, but aren't you crying this time so much?" asked the boy straightforwardly.

Facedown, hands on the knees, he was reciting the words of the testimony of faith,

ٱلتَّحِيَّاتُ لِلَّهِ وَٱلصَّلَوَاتُ وَٱلطَّيِّبَاتُ، ٱلسَّلَامُ عَلَيْكَ أَيُّهَا ٱلنَّبِيُّ وَرَحْمَةُ ٱللَّهِ وَبَرَكَاتُهُ، ٱلسَّلَامُ عَلَيْنَا وَعَلَىٰ عِبَادِ ٱللَّهِ ٱلصَّالِحِينَ، أَشْهَدُ أَنْ لَا إِلَٰهَ إِلَّا ٱللَّهُ، وَأَشْهَدُ أَنَّ مُحَمَّدًا عَبْدُهُ وَرَسُولُهُ

Translation: Salutations to God and prayers and good deeds. Peace be upon you, O Prophet, as well as God's mercy and His blessings. Peace be upon us and upon the righteous servants of God. I bear witness that there is no deity but God, and I bear witness that Muhammad is His servant and His messenger.

Tears were streaming down his cheeks towards his chin and wetting the bottom of his shirttail, like pearls, pure crystalline pearls.

"Uncle, the guests are waiting; they are looking fatigued."

They both were sitting silent, seeing the scenario that was somehow soothing their hearts. They didn't know why a sobbing vista caressed their skin like a cool summer breeze, smoothing their souls, taking away their jagged edges.

After moving his wet face to the right, uncle moved his face to the left and recited,

"ٱلسَّلَامُ عَلَيْكُمْ وَرَحْمَةُ ٱللَّهِ.

Translation: Peace be upon you, and the mercy of Allah.

Uncle raised his hands for the prayer (dua), wiped his wet face with the hands, and then stood up. His face was red; he glanced at the two girls whose heads were down. He couldn't see their faces.

"Ali," he said to the boy, "Thank you very much for bringing my guests here. I will surely reward you in return if Allah wills it. You may go now and play. Don't forget to tell the chef to bring something to eat."

"Okay, Uncle," he nodded his head in affirmation and went.

Uncle Umar said nothing but just sat on the sofa in front of them and waited for them to move their heads upward.

******

"Sorry to say, but I couldn't recognize you," Uncle broke the silence when he saw that they both weren't doing their heads up.

"We also don't know you," replied Zaini dismally with her head down.

(Why weren't they doing their heads up? Was it guilt? The guilt of what? Was it shame? Shame of what?)

"But Ali had said that my relatives had come!" he said anxiously.

"Yes, but," sighed Zaini, "It was a lie," and moved her head upward.

He didn't answer. Instead, he kept staring at them blissfully.

"It wasn't a lie, Zany; it wasn't a lie," said Uncle after a minute of constant staring.

Abeeha moved her head up when she listened to what Uncle said. Zaini became shocked, and Abeeha was the same. They both were astonished, as they didn't expect this kind of response. It was unbelievable for them, and the same state was of Uncle Umar. They all didn't expect this kind of situation. Their eyes weren't accepting the reality; it was just startling for all of them.

Uncle stood up, his eyes glimmered with watery tears. They both didn't know what was happening. He walked up to Zaini slowly and pulled her closer to himself, wrapping his arms around her. His embrace was warm, and his big, strong arms seemed very protective when wrapped around her frail body. The fragrance was coming from his clothes, and it only took a few seconds for Zaini to realize that this moment was no less than heaven.

"Father? Is this you? Father?" asked Zaini with a trembling voice, her eyes dripped with tears.

"Yes, Honey, it's me," he sobbed and kissed her forehead.

They both were crying, crying like a child. The tears burst forth like water from a dam; they were spilling down on their faces. The world around them melted away as she squeezed him back, not wanting the moment to end.

"What has my child done to herself?" he asked with care, holding her face in his shaking hands.

"How did you recognize me at a glance?" asked Zaini in return.

"Who forgets his blood relations? Who forgets his own child? No matter how far we were and for how long we were apart and how big and different you became, you are always the same for me. You are my kid, my little Zany," he said and sat beside her. It was the time that made Zaini forget all the moments she suffered alone in pain.

"She is my student, Abeeha," Zaini introduced Abeeha happily while pointing at her.

"Abeeha!" he came in shock. "Seriously, is she Abeeha?" he tilted his head towards her.

"Yes," answered Zaini casually. "Why are you so shocked?"

"You are Abeeha!" he said with excitement. Abeeha didn't understand what was happening.

There was an explosion in his brain, the right sort, the type that carries more possibilities than he could be conscious of. He could feel it. It was going to be the moment he always had waited for. Whatever was ahead could be the fulfillment of his most significant praise.

"Is your full name Abeeha Zaliq?" he asked.

"Yes," she answered in hysteria.

It was a delicious moment where a father's face washed blank with excitement like his brain cogs couldn't turn fast enough to take in the information from his wide eyes. Every muscle of his body just froze before a grin crept onto his face. It soon stretched from one side to the other, showing every single tooth.

He took a deep breath, "Praise is to Allah."

"Father, what happened?" asked Zaini when she became unable to understand anything.

"My kid, I also don't know what's happening," he replied with joy.

Then when you feel yourself in a garden.

And a little dew on you.

When you are fuckingly feeling good,

Then ask yourself, why me then too!

******

A boy arrived with orange juices and the plates of strawberries. Their mouths watered the moment they spotted them—fresh crimson strawberries covered with a mountain of tangy-sweet whipped cream, rich grainy brown sugar covering the sweet. Those little strawberries were wonderfully fresh, filled with bright red color.

The strawberries plate sat there on the table where the sunrays reflected, reflecting the red spectrum. They were a work of art conjured from such tiny seeds, and each one was born to become so sweet.

He also brought a large square box with a glossy black cover.

He pried the lid off, Zaini's and Abeeha's mouths watering—dark chocolates filled with cherries, some with caramel.

Then he brought a plate of cookies. Now they both could remain no more focused on anything else. Just thinking of their tastes, fingers tingling, they breathed deeper as if they were inhaling the fragrance of the bakery, their lips creeping upward. The cookies were calling.

Then the last turn was of sandwiches. They were like some kind of Scooby-Doo sandwiches. The filling was layers of cheese and ham with lettuce and tomato; oozing from the sides was copious amounts of mayonnaise. It looked like you'd need a flip-top head to eat it, or else you'd need to dislocate your jaw like a snake, but even then it looked yummy.

Uncle Umar glanced at both of them whose mouths were watering and who were licking their fleshy lips; he smiled.

"What are you waiting for!" he said smilingly.

"Father, we are literally so hungry," said Zaini childishly and took a cookie.

"Abeeha! Why aren't you taking anything?" asked Uncle. "You seem pretty uncomfortable!"

"No...Everything is fine. I am not hungry," lied Abeeha.

"Yummmmyyyy! The strawberries are perfect pockets of sweetness, softly fragranced for the taste buds," said Zaini joyfully. "Abeeha, why aren't you hungry? You should be more hungry than me; stop lying," she said funnily.

"Sorry, but...I don't want to eat," responded Abeeha hesitantly.

"Are you feeling like you are at a stranger's home? That's why you are not feeling good to eat?" asked the uncle.

"Somehow...Yes," replied Abeeha.

"I am not a stranger, Dear. I am your grandfather also," he reflected a sad smile.

"But I don't have any grandfather!" stated Abeeha.

"Oh Abeeha, he means that as he is my grandfather, so is yours. Father doesn't mean that he is your real grandfather," said Zaini with her mouth filled with a sandwich. "Now, eat; the food is so much delicious."

"No, Zany, I am her real grandfather," said Father, and Zaini's chewing mouth stopped.

His words surprised both of them; shock appeared on both faces. They were staring at him in awe, waiting for him to tell something more.

******

THE UNVEILING OF MAT

"So..." he thought about how to start their tangled story. "Let me tell you from the beginning, but you both also continue eating."

"Okay," said Zaini and continued chewing the sandwich bite that was in her mouth already. Abeeha also took a piece of sandwich.

"As Zaini, you know, and Abeeha, you don't, I am father of Ibrahim. I looked after him from the time he was of 4 as her mother, my wife died of cancer. Ibrahim married a Muslim woman named Khadija. From her womb were born two girls named Zaini and Abeeha. You both are the daughters of Ibrahim and Khadija, you both are sisters!" mentioned Father. Their eyes became wide, mouths remained open, not in a condition to say anything. "But your father Ibrahim loved a Hindu woman named Alisha. He wanted to marry her and wanted her to be his second wife. He was stubborn, and being a Hindu woman, I couldn't let him marry her.

Consequently, one day, he married her and brought her here at home without letting anyone know. Everyone was so shocked, and in that shock, your mother died with a heart attack. That time, Zaini was around 7 years old, and Abeeha was not of even a year. I even that time kept telling him to leave her, leave Alisha and marry some other Muslim girl. But instead of listening to me, after one or two months, he left me, left home, left this country, and went to Pakistan. That was the last time I saw my lovely son," his voice quivered.

"So, if we are sisters, why were we living in different houses?" asked Abeeha curiously.

"Alisha! Your stepmother refused to look after you as you were so small. She gave you to the orphanage, and there, you were adopted by the people you are living with. That's it, I don't know anything else," he took a deep breath.

Zaini remembered the pictures she found from the drawers. She had decided to find the corresponding point, and now she got to know. Additionally, she had also got the answer of who she really was in terms of religion. Her dad, father, and forefathers all belonged to Islam.

"Has he never met you since?" asked Zaini.

"After 4 or 5 years, he wrote me a letter. And then, he wrote to me many times, called and texted me a lot, but I didn't answer him even once 'coz I was waiting for him to come back. And now, I do regret it!" stated Father. "He once told me in his letter that you are adopted by a woman named Malika who lives with her daughter Maliha and a husband named Zaliq; that's how I got to know your full name," he told Abeeha. "Why didn't Ibrahim come with you? How is he now?" he asked Zaini. "Has he sent you both here?" he looked at both of them with hope.

She said nothing, just saw him, whose eyes were longing to see a moment that would make his whole being sparkling, whose eyes were waiting for a surprise that he was always wishing for, that his beloved son returned back and granted him a surprise like Boo justlike he used do in his childhood. Whose ears were longing to hear something good, something positive and whose whole existence was not willing to bear some bad news.

"Why aren't you answering?" he asked with panic.

"Sorry, Father, but he is no more," they were not the words that came out of her mouth. They were the arrows that came out of the bow and shattered his heart.

He gripped on so tightly even though his palms were soaring. His nails dug deep onto the corroded strings to give himself a better grasp. A tear rolled onto his cheek. He felt like an unquenchable fire that burnt all the oxygen in his body, leaving him listless and empty. It threatened to devour him, eat him whole and leave nothing but scraps behind.

The pain was like a knife being twisted in his spine, erasing every thought from his head and paralyzing his body. He struggled to stop his brain from listening to his voices. Small Ibrahim was kneeling—he remembered that—he fell and started crying. Ibrahim's father was ill, and Ibrahim was stroking his hair repeatedly, saying it would be all right with a voice that no one could have.

He sat there, tears pricking his eyes, pale hands trembling with grief and sadness. He had been trying to block out the screams, but it was impossible, the noise ripping his heart. Having the head in his hands, he was crying endlessly.

******

He was crying as if his brain was being shredded from the inside. Emotional pain flowed out of his every pore. From his mouth came a cry so raw that even the eyes of the boys and chefs around them were suddenly wet with tears. He grabbed onto a sofa so that his violent shaking body would not cause him to fall. And from his eyes came a thicker flow of tears than he had cried for even his own mother.

"Father!" vocalized Zaini. "Please stop crying."

"We expect the pain of the death of our parents, but never our child," he tried to put his shattering heart into words.

"Father, I do remember; you used to say that whatever happens is for good," she was also seizing herself so that she wouldn't burst into tears. She was also missing her dad a lot.

"To come so close to pure love and lose it so violently is something no medication can heal. I have been living from the day he left in the hope that he would return," he tried to stop the flow of his tears; somehow, he succeeded.

"Father, we are with you now. We will never leave you. Promise. Zaini and Abeeha, daughters of Ibrahim Umar," committed Abeeha and sat beside him.

"Yes, we will never," repeated Zaini and sat on the other side of the father.

"Oh, my love," he spread his arms on them and kissed their foreheads one by one.

اللّٰهُ أَكْبَرُ

اللّٰهُ أَكْبَرُ

اللّٰهُ أَكْبَرُ

اللّٰهُ أَكْبَرُ

Translation: God is the greatest.

The voice boomed across the sky; it was the Islamic call to prayer, Azaan recited by the muezzin. It was Zuhr. (One of the five Islamic mandatory Salah, the second prayer of the day.) Each person in that house became silent.

أَشْهَدُ أَنْ لَا إِلٰهَ إِلَّا ٱللّٰهُ

أَشْهَدُ أَنْ لَا إِلٰهَ إِلَّا ٱللّٰهُ

Translation: I bear witness that there is no God but Allah.

The voice was unexpectedly heart- soothing; the voice was powerful enough to make their bones feel like they were vibrating.

أَشْهَدُ أَنَّ مُحَمَّدًا رَسُولُ ٱللَّهِ

أَشْهَدُ أَنَّ مُحَمَّدًا رَسُولُ ٱللَّهِ..........

Translation: I bear witness that Muhammad is the messenger of Allah...

In 7 minutes, the Azan ended, and as soon as it ended, Father stood up.

"What are you doing?" asked Zaini.

"Preparation for the Salah," told Father.

"Is it necessary?" interrogated Zaini.

"Yes, Allah Ta'ala obligated it on us."

"Who Allah Ta'ala?" she questioned.

"Zaini!!!" he became surprised by hearing her question.

"Wait, wait... Are you saying that the helper is Allah?" asked Zaini again.

"Yes, the helper is Allah," he nodded in affirmation.

"Okay, and what is Salah?"

He took a deep breath. He understood that as her stepmother belonged to Hinduism, she didn't receive any Islamic education from her home.

"Abeeha, do you know what Salah is?" he asked her.

"I have seen people offering Salah, but I have never offered. I don't know what it is actually," she replied.

"Okay, you could also ask whatever you want to," he stated. "We are the souls that are created by Allah and then embodied in our mother's wombs. Somehow, we came into this form of being that included our spirit that Allah created but put in these earthly bodies. We have a passage for coming to this earth. We are placed out here with embodied souls, and that body can be a great ally for us and doing good. It's our companion in this life, and this is why the embodied prayer is such an important part of who we are," he stopped for a while and then continued when he found that they both were listening to him carefully. "Salah, prayer, and embodied prayer all somehow mean the same. Prayer is also called remembrance, and it's remembering who we are and why we are here, who we are, in relation with our Creator. The Creator..."

"Wait, wait," said Zaini. "The Creator is the helper, and the helper is Allah. Am I right?"

"Yes, you are, Honey," he affirmed.

"Okay, now continue," she giggled like a small kid.

"The Creator..." he glanced at Zaini and smiled affectionately. "The Creator of all things and this is the major distinction between Muslims and non-Muslims. We Muslims are in relation with Allah in Salah, prayer. We are connected to him in Salah, and who of us don't want to be connected with Allah, the creator, the King of everything?"

"Everyone wants to," answered Abeeha.

"Correct! But apart from the connection with the Creator, although that's part of it, embodied prayer is not just bringing good thoughts, although that's also important. It's bringing all of who we are in this life," he explained.

"Okay, so now I got to know that what is Salah or prayer, but why is it important?" asked Zaini.

"Do you want to shine?" he asked her.

"Of course, who does not?" she replied.

" For the shining of our souls, we need to offer Salah regularly throughout our lives. Hadhrat Abu Hurairah (Radhiyallaho anho) narrates that once the Prophet (Sallallaho alaihe wasallam) asked his companions..."

"May I ask you a thing?" queried Abeeha.

"Yes, sure."

"Prophet Muhammad (Sallallaho alaihe wasallam) is the last messenger of Allah Ta'ala, and Allah's messengers are those who convey Allah's message to the people, am I right?" she asked.

"Yes, you are absolutely right," he appreciated.

"And we are the followers of Hazrat Muhammad (Sallallaho alaihe wasallam)," Zaini added.

"Correct," he declared.

He got to know that they both had a few Islamic teachings. Maybe they got it from their environment, as Pakistan is an Islamic country. They just needed to revise those Islamic teachings and act upon them to become a Muslima from a Momina.

"Hadhrat Abu Hurairah (Radhiyallaho anho) narrates that once the Prophet (Sallallaho alaihe wasallam) asked his companions, 'Do you believe that dirt can remain on a person bathing five times a day in a brook running in front of his door?' 'No,' replied the companions, 'No dirt can remain on his body.' The Prophet (Sallallaho alaihe wasallam) remarked: 'So, exactly similar is the effect of Salat offered five times a day. With the Grace of Allah, it washes away all the sins," he stated the hadith of Hazrat Muhammad (Sallallaho alaihe wasallam). "Now, it's prayer time; I need to go," he said and stood up.

"But how do we know when to pray, how to pray, and in which direction we should pray?" asked Zaini.

"I will tell you after coming back."

"Where are you going?" she questioned again.

"To the mosque," he replied.

"Do we need to?" this time, Abeeha asked.

"No, women stay at home for offering Salah. Men go to the mosque for offering Salah," he declared.

"Okay, then bye," said Zaini.

Father smiled and went. Zaini was excited. The same condition was of Abeeha; questions about who she is in terms of religion concerned her also, but she never asked them.

And sometimes, the hardships that come in our lives can be a blessing in disguise. It is just our way of seeing and understanding the situations in our life.

******

Father returned after offering Salah in 30 minutes. Till then, they both kept gossiping, eating, and enjoying each other's company. After all, they both had formed a sisterhood, a safe space in which they could be utterly female without the gaze of an unknown cruel man.

And if the sisters aren't there to pick up and heal the shattered pieces, one can get trapped for years rather than winning the battle, which should be fought together.

"You both didn't tell me how did you come here in the case that you both didn't know me?" he asked while closing the door of the room. His eyes and nose were red; maybe he came after crying a lot. "And what have you two done to yourself? Why don't you both look at yourself at least!" he said in a quiet scolding manner, but that scolding was the one of love.

"Father, leave it first. Tell us more about Salah," said Zaini.

"No, first tell me why you both are in this weird condition?" he demanded again.

"Father, we are enjoying this kind of talk with you; please continue," insisted Abeeha.

"Okay, okay, seems that you have to be obeyed," declared father.

"Yes, you have to!" giggled Abeeha.

"Now, ask what you want to," he said.

"Okay, so…How do we know when to pray?" asked Abeeha.

"As you are here, in a Muslim community, you will hear the Azan that is the call to the prayer recited by the muezzin. It is like an indicator to call people towards prayer, towards Salah."

"So the muezzin recites Azan when he wants? No fixed timings!" asked Zaini, stunned.

"No, no, Dear," he denied. "The muezzin recites Azan according to the prayer timings, and the prayers are timed according to the movement of the sun."

"I have seen people offering Salah in different timings; I am unable to understand why they offer this way?" inquired Zaini.

"Dear, listen. We are obliged to offer Salah five times a day. There is a reason Allah told us to pray not once, or twice, or even three times but five times a day. It's because of focusing on Allah (Subhanahu wa ta'ala). It shifts our focus from whatever work we happen to be doing at that moment, whatever problem we happen to be in. No matter what your situation is, you still need to turn and pray. It means that you are at work, leave your employment, and focus on Allah (Subhanahu wa ta'ala). Whether you are at the mall, you leave that sale, and you focus on Allah (Subhanahu wa ta'ala). You are on your laptop, your phone, you leave that laptop, that phone, Facebook, meetings, class, whatever it is, and you focus on Allah (Subhanahu wa ta'ala). Allah is training us to focus on him and not on whatever it is we are doing in the world (Dunya)," told the father briefly. "And the timings are fixed according to the sun's movement. Our first prayer occurs before the sun comes up until the light fills the sky. It has many nuances. But right now, you could just simply understand that the first prayer occurs before the sun comes up until the light fills the sky, and that is called the Fajar prayer. Our second prayer is after the sun reaches the sky's highest point, called the Zuhr prayer. Then we have a late afternoon prayer before the sunset, and that is the Asar prayer. Our fourth prayer is Maghrib when the evenings become dark, and the fifth prayer is when the full darkness sets, that is Esha prayer," defined father.

"That means that the timings of prayers change every day because of the movement of the earth," stated Abeeha.

"Of course, during the year, as the earth moves around the sun, the sunrise's and the sunset's timings change every single day. And of course, this is like the calendar of our life. You know no day is the same as the one that comes before. So, we have to pay attention. If we are doing everything the same today as we did yesterday, we haven't grown, and that's a problem. The purpose of life is growth, so these movements of the prayer around the calendar as the earth moves around the sun should be a sign for us that we need to pay attention every day to what has changed," he described.

"Now, just a last question," requested Abeeha.

"Yes, yes, sure, no problem," answered Father.

"I have seen people washing some parts like hands, particularly face and some other parts before offering Salah. Why they do that? Is it a part of Salah?" she asked.

"Emm...You are asking about ablution (wudhu). It must be done before Salah as it is the first step of the preparation for the embodied prayer. Ablution, ritual ablution—to take pure water and wash face, wash hands including elbows, the top of the head, the feet and wash everything in a certain order. Keep this thing in your mind that I am just telling you everything superficially. I will later tell you the details," he declared. "And you know what? this ablution is an opportunity for us to wash away our sins! Isn't it amazing?" he asked.

"Seems pretty amazing, but how?" asked Abeeha in return.

"This is an opportunity to wash ourselves and our misdeeds with a strong intention," he said brightly. "So here again, physical action is reflected on the spiritual level. Isn't it a cheap and easy way to purify ourselves?" he asked.

"Are you sure this ablution could make us pure?" asked Abeeha in surprise.

"Yes, surely it could," he asserted. "Hadhrat Abu Uthman (Radhiyallaho anho) says: "I was once sitting under a tree with Hadhrat Salman (Radhiyallaho anho). He caught hold of a dry branch of the tree and shook it till all its leaves fell off. He then said to me, '0 Abu Uthman! (Radhiyallaho anho) Will you not ask me why I am doing this?' 'Do tell me,' I entreated. He said, 'The Apostle of Allah had done exactly like this before me while I was with him under a tree. He caught a dry branch of it and shook it, till all its leaves fell off.' At this, he said: '0, Salman! (Radhiyallaho anho) Will you not ask me why I am doing this?' I replied: 'Do tell me why you are doing this?' He remarked: 'Verily, when a Muslim does wudhu properly and then observes his Salaat five times a day, his sins fall off just as these leaves have fallen off.' He then recited the following verse of the Holy Qur'an: 'Establish Salat at the two ends of the day and at the approach of the night. Verily, good deeds annul ill deeds. This is a reminder for the mindful. (XI:114)'" he stated one of the hadith.

"Just ablution is required for the Salah?" a question bothered Zaini.

"No, not just ablution. There are many things that are required like standing in the right direction," he said.

"And what is the right direction?" she asked.

"All Muslims pray in the direction of the Holy Kaaba, and this direction is called the Qiblah. The Holy Ka'aba has a very ancient and sacred history; it's a place where Muslims believe that Hazrat Ibrahim (Alaihissalam) came and reestablished monotheism in the region. He and his son Hazrat Ismail (Alaihissalam) famously rebuilt the Holy Kaaba. So, Muslims everywhere in the world will first need to figure out that in which direction the Kaaba is," he explained. "As we know while standing here, the direction of the Holy Kaaba is in the east," he showed them while standing in the east direction.

"I will learn each nuance of Salah, ablution, timing in a nutshell of Islam. It looks so much interesting, so much amazing," said Abeeha.

"I will too," added Zaini. "But could I? I am a sinner. Is it so late?" she asked hesitantly.

"No, Honey, it is never too late," he appreciated her. "Allah Ta'ala will never reject your penitence. When you seek forgiveness, He will never reject your repentance for as long as you are genuine, for as long as you are sincere. You know what, people come to you, and they say, 'Please forgive me,' and you say, 'No problem.' They do the same thing the next day. 'Please forgive me,' and you say, 'Okay, no problem.' They do the third day and say, 'Please forgive me.' You will be like, 'Wait What!, Who are you playing with here? This is now three times,' and then you will say, 'Okay, this is the last time.' They come the fourth day after doing the same thing, and say, 'Please forgive me, my sister,' and your response will be like, 'You want me to keep forgiving you, what is it? How can you keep on doing this?'" he gave an example. "But, my dear, I promise you, with Allah Ta'ala, if you are genuine and sincere and you promise not to repeat a sin, but somehow later on, that sin is repeated due to your human nature or your weakness, due to devil's plot or plan, don't lose hope go back to Allah. Seek forgiveness again and promise him again that you are not going to do that and Allah will forgive you again, and again, and again, and again and a million times. Stop falling into the devil's trap by thinking that Allah (Subhanahu wa ta'ala) will not forgive me because Allah Ta'ala said clearly in verse, the verse with the most amount of hope in the Quran. Allah says:

Translation: 'O my servants! Who have acted extravagantly against their own souls, do not despair of the mercy of Allah. Surely, Allah forgives the faults altogether. Surely, He is Forgiving, the Merciful.'"

"Allah is saying never lose hope in my mercy. Never lose hope in the mercy of Allah, for indeed Allah will forgive all our sins. He is most Forgiving, most Merciful. So, the first trap of devil is he makes you think, 'I have committed the sin one or two times, and therefore, it's over. No hope for me, I am gone, I am dejected.' Never think that way. Remember," he was explaining to her, and indeed, Zaini was in peace.

"THEN WHICH OF THE FAVOURS OF YOUR LORD WILL YOU DENY?" he whispered to himself.

"'It was definitely the favor as the Lord chose them for His worship. And surely, as the Lord is the most merciful, He will surely protect them from the hellfire and will surely open Heaven's doors for them," he thought.

That moment seemed that from now onwards, the days will invert the shadows, and lightness will grow into the dark. There was a certain sense of warmth, a fullness of soul and breath that was thankfulness.

******

"You both are looking tired," Spoke Father.

"Yes, we are somehow," replied Zaini tiredly.

"Maryam!" he called out a girl, a pretty girl appeared in a second.

The girl was wearing a headscarf that seemed to be her perfect complement, neither pastel nor flamboyant that reminded them of flowers. She wasn't beautiful in a classical way, with no flowing golden curls or ivory skin and no piercing green eyes. She was shorter than average and more extensive than a catwalk model, but she was stunning in her ordinariness. Something radiated from within that rendered her irresistible.

"Show them their room, and also offer some new branded clothes to my kids," he said the second phrase warmly.

They both went with Maryam. She switched on the lights and gave them the clothes. The clothes were of silk, green and white color and that was Zany's favorite. They changed the clothes and sat on the beds in the room. The walls were cream, but not like the stuff she poured in the coffee. The floor was dark walnut, and instead of the roller blinds at the windows, the rich velvet curtains hanged there that reminded them of moss.

"Now, you both may sleep...It seems that you both haven't slept for a long time. Usually, people cannot sleep in fatigue and anxiety, and you both seem to be suffering from it. I am giving the pills; it's best if you both fall asleep yourselves. Otherwise, take the pills," said Maryam, and deep down, they both seriously wanted the sleep of peace.

She left the room and returned after some time with pills and glasses of water. She placed them on the side table and said,

"You both could sleep peacefully; consider this as it is your own home," switching off the lights, she again left the room.

"Do we need to consider?" Zaini questioned herself as the walls they were surrounded by had the calligraphy paintings that Zaini had done with her father. Each image reflected a happy memory that she could never forget no matter how older she got. She sunk into the moments she would never want to escape. It wasn't just a house; it was a home.

It was four o'clock in the afternoon, but in the scorching temperature of the city, the room was surprisingly calm. Because of the velvety curtains that were hung on the room's windows, their place became somewhat darker and felt more relaxed.

Abeeha gulped down the pills with water. Without it, falling asleep would be impossible. There were many thoughts that it was complicated for her to lie down and wait for falling asleep. After a few minutes, she felt drowsiness on her nerves.

******

THE ULTIMATE VERDICT

The room was filled with darkness when she woke up. She got up from the bed and went to the wall where the switchboard was placed and turned on the night bulb. The wall clock showed half-past eleven. She could not sum up how she slept for so long and how her sister was still sleeping. Were they influenced by the pills or was it the consequence of not sleeping well for many days?

Whatever the reason was, she was feeling much better than before. She was feeling ravenously hungry, but she had no idea that the people of the house would be awake or not. She opened the door slightly and came to the lounge. Sitting on the sofa, Father was reading some book. Listening to the noise of the door opening, he looked up and smiled.

"Slept well or not?" he asked with delectation.

"Well..." she tried to smile.

"Now, go straight in the kitchen. Food will be there, heat it up and eat there on the table. Then make two cups of tea, one for you and one for me," he said with a smile as if a father would say to her daughter, with great affection.

She said nothing but did as he directed. After 15-20 minutes, she gave him the cup of tea. He put the book on the table. She sat on the sofa that was beside him with her teacup.

"Tea is good," he said smilingly after taking a sip.

Neither she smiled in return nor she thanked him. She just kept seeing him. She looked so much confused.

"What happened?" he asked while looking into her empty eyes.

"I have a question. Will you answer me truly?"

"Absolutely."

"Will the ablution surely make me pure?" she asked strangely.

"Of course," he became astonished at her question.

"Okay, thank you," she said with the same emptiness.

"Don't you believe?"

"How can a filthy girl like me be pure?" she asked sadly.

"Filthy!" he was surprised, "My baby is such a charming and beautiful girl."

"Yes," she sighed.

"What happened," he said with endearment.

"Nothing...I have a headache," she tried to change the topic.

"Need some more rest?"

"No...No need...Just give those pills from which I could sleep for a longer time, or...For forever," she completed her phrase hardly.

"Do you want to go home?"

"No...Never..."

"Then..." he waited for her to speak. "Any problem that is swirling in your head?"

"I say weird things sometimes, and it is always the effect of migraine. Sorry," she was talking unfamiliarly.

"I am a doctor, Abeeha!" he said with solemnity. "And I know this is not happening just because of migraine."

"What good would it do me if I told you? Will my messy head and my dirty self be pure?" she asked him reversely.

He didn't understand what to say. He didn't expect this kind of question.

"What happened, my child, my most beautiful baby? Why are you saying this for yourself?" he asked with admiration. "Has anyone bothered my girl?" he asked outwardly without even thinking what he was saying, and she became still on his words, unable to move.

"How do you say that? I mean, how do you know that?"

"Wait...What! Have you been bothered?" he asked again. His condition was as if someone had taken away his breath.

"Yes..." she was unable to comprehend why she didn't say, “No.”

He remained silent for a time, like trying to overwhelm his uncertainty.

"Who bothered you?"

"Zaliq," with the hatred that she held, she couldn't even spell him as dad.

"What, What did he do?"

And she started telling him, this time with no tears, but with the features born from thunder and battle, with the lips made of glass and a voice cut from steel.

She told him everything from the first day of her internal brokenness and crippled self until she was with him, from the destructive childhood till the awful escape. She told everything, and the one who was listening could not believe what tragic situations his lovely kiddos did suffer.

"Can you still say that I am beautiful enough?" This was the only question that whirled in her mind always.

"You are beautiful enough," he delineated.

"After knowing me totally, how could you say I am beautiful?" she was stubborn. "Do you ever just wonder how different everything would have beeen and how beautiful I would be if that one thing didn't happen to me?"

"My dear, life teaches you. Life never teaches everyone, and the chosen one who is taught by life becomes special. The disciples made by life grow prematurely. They become distinctive. They have the invaluable treasure given by life in the form of lessons. They are the most prominent and unique in the crowd of millions like the way you are." There was encouragement in his eyes, the way they were warm and soft. His words were few, yet she felt her more capable, more able, a better human than she otherwise could have ever been. "And I can tell you with full honesty that the most beautiful person in the world is my child, Abeeha. My dear, beauty does not mean blue eyes, long wavy chestnut-colored hairs, pastel white skin, pink lips, tenderly fingers, soft hands, spindly arms and legs, and slender body. You aren't a supermodel, but you have a beauty that made those billboard-princesses look as paper-thin as they are; you are something robust and real. 'Beautiful' is a casual smile that is so freely given. It is the soul's tenderness that makes a beautiful connection with others. 'Beautiful' is your soul, the one that loves so deeply and cares so very much for others. 'Beautiful' is a story of the innermost pages of your soul as that is what makes you BEAUTIFUL." He had a way of encouraging her to see all that she was capable of. Where others held her back or hit upon her self-esteem, he did the exact opposite. If they were chains, he was the key. He wanted her to have the same mental freedom he had, to see her strengths and build her stronger.

You are made of so much charm and grace,

But maybe you forgot;

When you believe in people's judgments,

And the things you are not.

"But it defines me!" said Abeeha.

"Nothing defines you, Dear, 'coz a definition excludes the possibility of change," he spoke, and this was the best answer she had ever got to any of her questions.

And when someone shows you real love, the kind of love that is dependable, endurable, sustainable, and above all, kind! Then you can let your spark burn brighter. After all, they are genuinely supporting you because they bring their own inner fire to love you. Their words will encourage you in a realistic way that helps you towards a sustainable emotional life and protects you from those who lost their spark and would seek to extinguish yours for little more than a toxic ego.

******

Zaini woke with the sound of breathing. It was the dream that woke her up. Her eyes took in every ray of light of the night bulb, and without a doubt, she knew she had slept too long.

Though her eyes were open, her heart was pounding, and her mind was empty. She was unable to think anything except the dream. It's as if a hypodermic of adrenaline had been emptied into her carotid.

She moved slowly enough to make no sound. She realized that she was standing nowhere in life; she felt her existence a burden. She would never stand on her own feet. She was feeling that she had wasted her entire life. What her dream was and where she stood.

She turned on the tube light and locked the door. There was a computer in the corner. She turned that on, sat on the chair, and as soon as the computer was on, she clicked on the YouTube icon and started searching for her dance video which had gone viral a long time ago.

She was scrolling YouTube with an empty mind when a lyric video of an English nasheed opened accidentally.

"I know I'm waiting

Waiting for something

Something to happen to me

But this waiting comes with

Trials and challenges

Nothing in life is free."

The voice was so gentle, or maybe the words were expressing her feelings.

"I wish that somehow,

You'd tell me out aloud.

That on that day, I'll be okay.

But we'll never know 'coz

That's not the way it works.

Help me find my way."

She had listened to many songs several times before, but she had never thought to listen to this nasheed and then sink into its words in this way.

"My Lord, show me right from wrong.
Give me light, make me strong.
I know the road is long.
Make me strong."

After having a dream of an elegant library of books, her only desire left was to study and become a scholar.

"Sometimes, it just gets too much.
I feel that I've lost touch.
I know the road is long.
Make me strong."

Zaini suddenly stood up from the chair and went toward the windows. She could see the black sky outside. There was a strange horror out and a peculiar terror inside.

"I know I'm waiting
Yearning for something
Something known only to me
This waiting comes with
Trials and challenges
Life is one mystery."

Standing there, through the window's glass, seeing the shiny stars in the dark sky, she was trying to come out of the emptiness.

"I wish that somehow,
You'd tell me out loud.
That on that day, you'll forgive me.
But we'll never know 'coz,

That's not the way it works.

I beg for your mercy."

"I will be a ballerina," she remembered the sentence frequently said for many years while listening to the nasheed and looked down as a loser. She didn't become a ballerina, and now her only desire was to become a scholar. "How could she become that now?" she looked outside. "Nothing is in man's hand?" she said to herself.

"My Lord, show me right from wrong.

Give me light, make me strong.

I know the road is long.

Make me strong.

Sometimes, it just gets too much.

I feel that I've lost touch.

I know the road is long.

Make me strong."

Zaini looked back at the computer's screen. The voice was so heart-soothing that she came and sat on the chair.

"My Lord, show me right from wrong.

Give me light, make me strong.

I know the road is long.

Make me strong

Sometimes it just gets too much.

I feel that I've lost touch.

I know the road is long.

Make me strong."

The man was chanting the last stanza repeatedly, and she opened another tab. Zaini's fingers were moving on the keyboard with thunderbolt speed. Each filled line of getting admission to Pakistan's university decreased her soul's emptiness. It was like coming out of a magic zone.

******

The black sky gradually turned into dim grey, and the illumination of stars got languidly lusterless. Millions of stars in the ebony sky started hiding their brightness and slowly dissipated as if someone was going to come. And after a long night, the sun came out victoriously of its abode across the brilliant orange horizon and glimmered in the sky.

The sparkling sun clearly differentiated the sky and the land. It rose like any other day, the daybreak brought glimmers of warmth. The golden light softly caressed the ground, and delicate yellows and reds filled the sky, perfectly reflecting the calm.

Divergent birds were gently flying in the manifest sky, and their dulcet dawn chorus was easily audible. A fleck of sunlight glittered on the windowpane, reflecting the light into the room. At that beginning of the day, Zaini came out of the room with a cute little face covered in a hijab. She had packed her luggage in a suitcase—luggage including the clothes, pairs of shoes, hairs, wigs, books, and hijabs.

Father and Abeeha both were still gossiping with each other while sitting on the dining table chairs, which was precisely infront of the room's door. As soon as Zaini opened the door, they became astonished by seeing her adorable face covered in a hijab.

"You are looking so pretty in this hijab," he glorified. "It's good that you got up, we were talking about you, and you know what? We have a piece of good news for you," he chirped.

"Good news? For me?" she sounded surprised. "What?"

"I have seen a handsome, well-mannered, and good-earning boy for your marriage," he said gladly.

"Marriage...?" stammered Zaini.

"Yes, and you know, he is so elegant. I have seen him; you may say that he is chestnut and the acorn, the seed of everything good to come, a brown-haired boy. He has eyes of pure obedience and a heart of gold. He has that way of moving that honest people do, with the spark of a smile that comes from the core of his soul," added Abeeha.

She kept seeing them with her frozen white face. What future she saw a minute ago and what fate they were showing her.

If she hadn't had confirmed her admission at the Pakistan university, she would have said yes, but now, she couldn't.

"But I can't marry."

"Why?" they both asked together.

"I was always a daisy in a world that only wanted a rose. So, I thought myself unworthy to grow as tall and wild as my heart needed to grow. Yet, when a daisy grows so big, she can hold her own next to any rose when she grows colorful as a vivid rainbow. And as a bonus, she lacks thorns. So when someone like you with a great heart encouraged you to grow as a daisy, that's when the potential found itself quite unlocked. So, I want to grow now. I first want to study," she apprised. "And I would study enough so that I would know the difference between good and bad, the difference between the things that are considered permissible and lawful under religion and the things that are forbidden and punishable according to Islamic law," she stated her excuse.

"Zany! We will always be here for you. Letting you marry doesn't mean that we are getting disassociated from you...You are my daughter," asserted Father and Zaini's eyes filled with water.

"Okay, I am not forcing you. If you want to study, then you can," permitted Father.

"Wait for some years, and then I will get married wherever you want," she said to Father. "But not right now."

"Where and what do you want to study?" he didn't force her more. Instead, he asked her about her studies.

"I have got admission in a university of Pakistan for becoming a scholar, and I have a flight tomorrow," she said, and both of them became whammy.

"But...tomorrow...?" sputtered Abeeha.

"Don't worry about me, Abeeha. I just don't want to neglect the peace which I got after several years in acquiring the knowledge of Islam," she took a deep breath.

"You have made a good decision," said father after some moments.

Zaini smiled, went back to the room, and came back with a painting. It was a calligraphy painting.

"It is for you, Abeeha," Zaini gave that painting to Abeeha and smiled a bit.

"Can I come with you?" she asked abruptly, and she nodded her head in negation.

"Why?" Abeeha asked restlessly.

"This country needs a warrior, a survivor like you," she tried to make her understand something very deep in such a little phrase.

"I will wait for you," said Abeeha

Abeeha saw her with blurry eyes. Without saying anything, she hugged her and started sobbing. Zaini was also weeping under the siege of her arms.

******

CHEERIO

She packed the last few things she had in the room with tears streaming down her face. Leaving was her choice, but it was hard for her to leave the people who made her feel loved. She walked towards Father and Abeeha, and indeed, she was going to miss them the most. She hugged her father and sobbed into his chest.

She hugged Abeeha, who was already sobbing. Abeeha didn't want to let her sister, her teacher, her life-changing source to go because she thought that if she let her go, she won't be able to hold her again.

"I don't know how I'm supposed to live without you now," she whispered. "I want you to promise that you will be with me whenever I am scared so that I could hold your hands."

"I promise I will be if Allah wills," said Zaini and smiled while looking at her father.

Abeeha looked nowhere but started holding Zaini's hand. Zaini looked at her, confused.

"What are you scared of?" asked Zaini.

"I am scared if I let your hand go, you will disappear," As soon as Abeeha completed her sentence, Zaini forgot to breathe.

"I'll always pray for you, and that's how I will be there with you even if you won't be able to see me. I'll always be there,"

Zaini said after a moment and Abeeha got the slightest glimmer of hope.

Abeeha held Zaini's hands and put a paper in her hands. "This is for you," she said and closed those hands.

"What is this?" asked Zani while opening the folds of that paper.

"In such a hurry, I was unable to give an incredible gift to you, so I just composed a poem," mentioned Abeeha.

I wish I could hold you tight,

And don't let you go.

But my arms aren't strong enough

To hold on to you for long.

Zaini started reading the poem aloud.

I wish I could hold you tight

And don't let you go

But my arms aren't strong enough

To hold on you for long

So, I wish I could hold your heart

Carefully as if in a cradle

And see what I don't understand

So. I could retain my patience

My eyes have seen a lot of things

But I wish I could see yours

The things you are going through

And ignite them once and all

I could feel the way you call me kid
Like the echoing waves of a shore
The way you see me in a glance
Makes me believe there is so more
This heart existing in my chest
Have stood collecting dust
But yes, I found a gate of you
That leads right to my trust
I have never really loved myself
But you have loved me whole
You let me see the sparkling light
That exists in my soul
I promise I will let you see
A fantastic version of me
'Coz your heart deserves so much more
Than a broken girl like me.

Zaini's voice trembled while reading the last few lines. She looked into her eyes and said, "Words end to describe, Abeeha, how beautiful and loving this poem is. Love you a lot," she tried to narrate her emotions but failed. It wasn't enough. "I love you more," she replied and left her hands, not wanting to cry more.

"Father...!" she looked at her father who was standing beside Abeeha.

"Kid, try not to think of the leaving part because there is no stronger glue in all the known universe than true love. And I see in your heart and mind that it is what we share. Love is the only path we should follow, so don't think of this as abandonment, sweet child. Know that it is the only sure way to stay together," spoke Father. "Now go!"

"Okay, I am going, Assalamu Alaikum," at her salam, they all smiled.

"Walaikumassalam. Take care." With one last tear shedding down his face, he let her go. This was it. This was goodbye. She ambled her way to the door, and before she grabbed onto the handle, she looked back one last time, wishing this would just all be a dream though saying goodbye was her own will. It wasn't a dream. It was reality.

Zaini stepped out of the door, a welcoming aroma tickled her nose, and her eyes flew up. As she stepped onto the road, the chirrups of the beautiful birds, the light, and the breeze greeted her a good day ahead. The morning was bright and mesmerizing as it was inviting her to stare deep into the horizon. She thought of how loving it is that the beginning of a new day resembles hope and the promise of adventure.

She came out of the things strongly and came out wiser too. She still has her loving heart and always has her idealism and courage. She even could take forward leaps whether she could see the ground or not. But this heart, it's not for everyone. It's not for the ones who threw the knives, forgiven though they are.

******

But in the end, we truly realize we all have gone through black and white.

THE DEFINITIVE TEST

My brothers and sisters, this place is designed to break our hearts. It was intended that way. You are not the servant of 'Eesa' (Jesus) or 'Krishna' or 'Ganesh'; you are not the servant of fashion or money or fame or beauty or power or position. You are the slave of Allah (Subhanahu wa ta'ala), and Allah has chosen you from amongst billions of human beings. Allah (Subhanahu wa ta'ala) has promised that he will test us, and he will test us with so many different things. One of them is patience. Allah (Subhanahu wa ta'ala) wants us to be patient, and Allah will put in our lives certain things that will test us. And this is why in Surah Aal-e-Imran verse number 142, Allah SWT tells us:

Translation: Do you really think that you will be granted entry into Paradise and Allah has not yet tested you, who from amongst you is truly prepared to struggle for the sake of Allah SWT and who is patient?

There will be hardships, there will be difficulties, which is the reality of life, but pain and sufferings only become harmful when they create a barrier between us and Allah (Subhanahu wa ta'ala). The pain becomes positive, motivating when it brings us back to Allah (Subhanahu wa ta'ala). We have to realize that everything which is happening is from Allah, but we forget about Allah's presence. We forget about Allah's power, we forget that we came from a clot; we were nothing. We get so afraid because we forget Allah (Subhanahu wa ta'ala). We fear and forget that everything is in Allah's control. Indeed, we will be tested; each and every single one of us will be tested either with a loss of wealth, loss of life, loss of profit, and trade. So, give glad tidings to those who are patient when they are tested.

Allah (Subhanahu wa ta'ala) says we are gonna test all of you to distinguish between you. If you are patient, you will achieve contentment. If you are lazy, you will not achieve pleasure. If you are ready to work hard and struggle for the sake of Allah (Subhanahu wa ta'ala), you will definitely achieve contentment. So, my brothers and sisters, remember that whatever test is put into your life, bear patience, don't get depressed. If we forget about Allah, we end up getting depressed. We think things are in black, they're gloomy, no! No, we don't believe this. We believe in happy endings. No matter how bleak it looks out there, it's 'Dunya'[world]. We're in the lowest, Dunya means the lowest place. Dunya is on the bottom; there is only up from here. Really, there is only up, and we will make it through the test. We will be content, we will be happy. We will be in the pleasure of Almighty. It's not going to be comfortable, the Almighty did not promise us that our life would be easy, but He did promise us:

Translation: And if you bear patience, He will grant you contentment.

He will make us realize those who have less than us. He will make us apprehend so many things that we have been favored by Allah (Subhanahu wa ta'ala), and this is why Allah says that He wants to test us to know who is ready to struggle in His cause for His sake. We are lazy at the time, and that laziness gets us nowhere. Are you prepared to put in effort into pleasing Allah (Subhanahu wa ta'ala)?

******

HOW TO GAIN CONTENTMENT?

Allah (Subhanahu wa ta'ala) speaks one of the necessary qualities for us to gain closeness to Him, and it's a sign of Allah's mercy.

The first quality is leniency, leniency in one's character. Don't be harsh, don't be hard-hearted: soften your heart, be indulgent and be soft in general. Especially with the people and your interaction with them, because Allah (Subhanahu wa ta'ala) says in verse number 159 of Surah Aal-e-Imran:

Translation: It's because of the mercy of Allah (Subhanahu wa ta'ala) that you're lenient with those around you (O Messenger Muhammad Sallallaho alaihe wasallam.)

Obviously, the lesson is for every one of us. It is the sign of the mercy of Allah that we become lenient towards those around us, and Allah (subhanahu wa ta'ala) says:

Translation: If you are harsh and hard-hearted, they would have dispersed from amongst you. So, forgive them and seek forgiveness for them and consult them in the affairs.

If we are to consult those around us, those of importance, our parents, and those who mean a lot to us regarding essential matters in our lives, and even those we have no relation, it will make us one of the people who are much more content.

Similarly, if we forgive people and we pray for them, it will make us content. We hold grudges, and we curse people; that's why we lose contentment. We need to learn to let things go—we are talking about humankind's general issues. We must let something go as far as possible. We must pray for the people who have harmed us, the people who are around us; when we do that, we achieve contentment. This is not a joke; it's difficult, it's really, really tough. But if we are prepared for this, Allah promises us that we will be successful.

As part of that success, we will achieve happiness, peace because it is a sign of Allah's mercy. So leniency remembers not to be harsh, hard-hearted. Remember to forgive people, remember to pray for people, and remember to consult people as well. This is extremely important, and it is the blessing of Allah (Subhanahu wa ta'ala). In verse number 190 of Surat Aal-e-Imran, Allah (Subhanahu wa ta'ala) tells us something that will bring lots of satisfaction.

Translation: Indeed, in the creation of the skies and the earth, the heavens and the earth, and in the movement of the day and the night, there are signs for those with sound intellect. Those who remember Allah while they are standing, while there are seated, while they are lying down and they are pondering over the signs of Allah in His creation.

Allah (Subhanahu wa ta'ala) encourages us to ponder over His creations. There are signs for those with sound intellect. That is why take a moment to go out with your family, with those who are beloved to you. Go out to see the nature with the intention of witnessing the creation of Allah to understand his greatness and grandeur. This is Allah. His creature is so massive, so sophisticated. Imagine Allah Himself; imagine how tremendous and powerful He is. Sit and ponder over oceans and how blue they are. Look at the greenery, look at the mountains and how great they are. Look at the forests, look at the animals, look at the various other creatures of Allah (Subhanahu wa ta'ala), the clouds, the wind, rain, whatever else they may be, and ponder over the greatness of Allah (Subhanahu wa ta'ala). Look at the ants and the other minute creatures, how sophisticated they are, and how they work. We will achieve closeness to Allah (Subhanahu wa ta'ala) in all of this, and definitely the contentment.

Many of us need a break...My brothers and sisters, when we go for a break, and we go on a holiday, our intentions need to be rectified and fine-tuned. We are going, yes: we will enjoy ourselves. We will enjoy ourselves within what the Almighty has ordained and permitted, but at the same time, we want to see the creations of Allah. We want to see what Allah (Subhanahu wa ta'ala) has made, and that will bring about the urge within us to remember Allah. That is why looking at Allah's creation without remembering Him is a waste of time, but to look at it is to be in owe. Look at the greatness of Allah; this will bring about comfort in the heart.

My brothers and sisters, that will translate into contentment in our entire life. So, when we go out for a little while to witness and to watch whether it is to the lake or to the ocean or whether it is to the desert or to the forest, whatever else it is, remember this point and, InshaAllah, it will bring about much contentment. Allah (Subhanahu wa ta'ala) says, "Everyone will be tested; don't compare what you have and what others have been given. You don't know what Allah has taken away from them."

We often look at what Allah (Subhanahu wa ta'ala) has bestowed upon people and feel unfortunate, but we don't know what Allah took away from them. So, don't compare. Allah (Subhanahu wa ta'ala) tells us in verse number 200 in the same surah, Surah Aal-e-Imran, a very significant fact, which is also connected to forbearance and patience:

Translation: O you who believe! Bear patience, bear even greater patience, learn to protect the limits of Allah (Subhanahu wa ta'ala), and be conscious of Allah. Develop your relationship with Allah in order that you may achieve success.

So that's the fascinating verse connected to patience. The last verse I want to speak about with all of the readers is verse number 17 of Surah An-Nisa where Allah says:

Translation: Repentance is for the one who has committed the sin in ignorance and returns to Allah in repentance very quickly soon after that.

This means that repent to Allah as soon as you commit the sin, and you will achieve contentment. If you leave it, you actually dig yourself deeper and deeper into the vice, and you turn further and further away from Allah. You want contentment, you must turn to Allah soon after committing sin. If you have Allah, you have everything you desire. If you don't have Allah, nothing will make you happy, nothing! It will all and then bring you misery, Wallahi [by allah], that's the truth.

May Allah forgive us and grant us contentment.

******

TO DEAR READERS

I hope that you find yourself in one of this book's pages. I am trying to give birth to the words that are engraved in my soul. I honestly hope you find the courage to climb over the obstacles in your way after reading this book.

ACKNOWLEDGMENTS

In the first instance, I thank Allah Almighty for everything, as, without His help, nothing could be done.

Writing a book is not work done in a snap of fingers, but I have been very fortunate to have an army of supporters along my way. Nobody has been more important to me in the pursuit of this book than the members of my family. My heartfelt thanks go to my family, a teacher, and a friend who are great collaborators and supporters for me. I would have abandoned this book altogether, but their fierce support and nurturing gave me the confidence to write an influential book. They gave wise advices and much encouragement. They all are the ultimate role models. Thanks to all the beautiful people who allow me to carry on their torch and spread their flame through the world like wildfire.

May Allah bless us all.

Ameen.

ABOUT THE AUTHOR

Binte Tahir is a sixteen-year-old author, writes poetries in English, Urdu, and Arabic. Born in Karachi, Pakistan, she belongs to an open-minded family. She dreamed of a charming future but, early on, something frowned upon in her middle-class household. She moved along some hardships, which left her with post-traumatic stress disorder for some years of her life. This marked a transition in her early life from one carefree childhood to one filled with relative uncertainty. Despite her life being dogged by some adversities, she is very generous and has dreamed of an artistic career. She began to ferment social and domestic life ideas, injustice, and a need for retaining the child as a child, not an adult.

As well as being a humanistic novelist, she always tries to become a humanitarian in real life. She brings the real-life characters and the modern era obstacles in her novel to make the book readers, especially the one who mentally love to live in an academy that smells wood and old books at the head of a secret society, aware of the joys of real life. She writes realistically about children tackling problems and experiencing emotions that readers could empathize with. She wants to technically arrange the ink lines on a page to make the readers feel the same feelings they felt in their real lives.

Printed and Bound by ***Passive Printers*** - www.passiveprinters.com
Printing press that offers Print on Demand (POD) Facility.
Printed in The Islamic Republic of Pakistan.

www.ingramcontent.com/pod-product-compliance
Lightning Source LLC
LaVergne TN
LVHW091305150826
845673LV00006B/1539

* 9 7 8 9 6 9 7 4 9 1 1 5 5 *